D1483688

WINDOWS OF THE
SOUL

WINDOWS OF THE SOUL

A MAN'S PRACTICAL GUIDE TO MASTERING HIS EYES

RABBI ZVI MILLER

EDITED BY:
Charlotte Friedland
Yehudit Channen

COVER DESIGN:
Ruti Schleider

PAGE LAYOUT AND DESIGN:
Eden Chachamtzedek

ISBN 978-965-91355-1-6

First printing, 2009
Second printing, 2010
Third Printing, 2014

Copyright © 2009
by Rabbi Zvi Miller

PUBLISHED BY:
Kol Publishers
A Levado Group Company, New York

IN CONJUNCTION WITH:
The Salant Foundation
10/11 Nachal Lachish St.
Ramat Beit Shemesh, ISRAEL
salant@netvision.net.il

Printed in Israel

לעילוי נשמת

In Memory of

Michael ben Altoon

Eliyahu ben Sulcha

Esther bat Leah

Rachel bat Margalit

תנצב"ה

בס"ד

שמואל קמנצקי
Rabbi S. Kamenetsky

2018 Upland Way
Philadelphia, Pa 19131

Home: 215-473-2798
Study: 215-473-1212

Rabbi Mattisyahu Salomon

ר"ח שבט תשס"ט לפ"ק

דוד המלך cries out in תהלים קי"ט

"פלגי מים ירדו עיני על לא שמרו תורתך"

My eyes have shed streams of tears because they did not keep your תורה.

רבינו יונה points out that דוד המלך doesn't say because *I* did not keep your תורה but rather because *they* did not keep your תורה.

They refer to the eyes!

The root of tragedy is that the *eyes* didn't keep the תורה.

Everything starts with the eyes, those wonderful organs that can do so many valuable things, but can also do so much dreadful damage!

Therefore we owe a tremendous debt of gratitude to הר"ר צבי מילר שליט"א for investing so much effort in providing such a practical guide on this sensitive subject of שמירת עינים, to make אחינו בני ישראל aware of the great dangers to which they are all exposed, and to assist in combating them.

ובזכות עבודת הקודש למען קדושת מחנינו יזכה לשפע ברכה מן השמים

מתתי' חיים סלומון

(718) 436-1133

RABBI YAAKOV PERLOW
1569 - 47TH STREET
BROOKLYN N.Y. 11219

יעקב פרלוב
קהל עדת יעקב נאוואמינסק
ישיבת נאוואמינסק - קול יהודא
ברוקלין, נ.י.

בס"יד ה' דג"ו מנ"ל

Mr. David Ashear has shown me the
work "Wisdom of the Soul" written by Rabbi
Zvi Miller on the sensitive, but imperative,
subject of Shmiras Einayim. I have read it
and was very impressed by its clarity, Torah
concepts, and practical guidance for all men
in our society today.

The compelling challenges that observant Jews
face in the modern world make it absolutely important
that they fortify their minds and souls with Torah
instruction on these matters and apply it in
their everyday lives. "Wisdom of the Soul" is
an extremely helpful work in meeting this goal

Rabbi Yaakov Perlow

Rabbi Chaim Walkin

7 Kassuto St.
Jerusalem

הרב חיים וואלקין

רחוב קאסוטו 7
ירושלים

בס"ד

יום א' לסדר בא

ער"ח שבט תשס"ט

הנה ראיתי ספרו באנגלית של ידיד נפשי, הרה"ג ר' **צבי מילר** שיחי' שאני מכירו מקרוב, זה תקופה ארוכה. ואסף איש טהור, דברי חז"ל המלהיבים בעניני שמירת העיניים והנפש, וגם דוגמאות הלכה למעשה איך לישמר.

ויפה מאד עשה, ושכרו הרבה מאד, בפרט בתקופתינו אשר כמה מן החיזוק והשמירה צריך, ובפרט להנוער ובני תורה, שהשטן מתגרה בהם ביותר.

והנה ר' צבי הנ"ל הוא יקר יקרים, מלא בתורה וביר&ת שמים, וכל כוונתו בזה החיבור הוא לשם שמים.
כמה מן החובה לתומכו ולעוזרו בכל מה שניתן לעזור, ולקחת חלק בדבר הנשגב הזה.

והקב"ה יערה רוח טהרה ממרום על כל אלו שעוסקים בזה, ונזכה להרבות גבולי הקדושה והטהרה.

וע"ז באעה"ח

ברוב ידידות ויקר

חיים וואלקין

Rabbi Eliezer Harari   BS"D

15th Tevet, 5769

     I would like to commend Rabbi Zvi Miller and David Ashear on their undertaking to address the issue of שמירת עינים which literally affects all כלל ישראל.

     This book explains the difficulties and offers the reader practical suggestions, based upon Chazal, to overcome this problem.

     I feel that it is incumbent upon every person to familiarize themselves with the contents of this book.

     May this project be a זכות for the authors and a תועלת for the רבים.

Eliezer Harari

Rabbi Eliezer Harari

Congregation Ohel Simha
BUILDING FOR THE FUTURE

PO BOX 2088 · 295 PARK AVE — ELBERON, NJ 07740 TELEPHONE 732-571-2711 FAX 732-571-1491

בס"ד פרשת נשא

Rabbi
Rabbi Shmuel Choueka

Hazan
Haim Arking
Michael Safdieh

Executive Committee

President
Richard Shweky

Members
Steven Cornman
Michael Fallas
Eli Kairey
Ike Levy
David Mugrabi
Eddie Anteby
Isaac Saka
Charles Mamiye

Past Presidents
Abe Shamah
Raymond Beyda
Irwin Mizrahi
Michael Fallas
Eddie Anteby
Steven Cornman

I was very pleased to see the new book "Windows of the Soul" by Rabbi Zvi Miller, which enables a person to guard his eyes and gain self control in a very important area. But I was more excited knowing that this came about through the idea of a very special person, Mr. David Ashear, who persevered and nurtured this from a dream to a reality.

As we all know, this soul and hence the eyes, as the title suggests, must be safeguarded from spiritual pollution, which is rampant in today's society. This wonderful work, which will help one achieve this goal is remarkable and deserves our support.

May the author and my good friend David Ashear be blessed with the beracha of, וזרעם בכורים הרביה ונתת'יה

Sincerely,

Rabbi Shmuel Choueka

Contents

The Salant Foundation

Mussar: The Wisdom of Personal Growth

THE SALANT FOUNDATION provides access to the wisdom of Mussar through publications, eMussar (our daily email lessons), distance learning and live seminars.

We are honored to present, "Windows of the Soul," and sincerely hope that this guidebook will significantly help you master your eyes and add holiness to your life.

Following in the footsteps of Rabbi Yisrael Salanter zt"l, our vision is to help every member of Klal Yisrael study Mussar on a daily basis and strive for personal excellence.

To sign up for our eMussar series send an email to salantorg@gmail.com

Warmest blessings,
Rabbi Zvi Miller
Dean

P.S. For questions or comments, contact Rabbi Zvi Miller at salantorg@gmail.com.

Acknowledgments

LAST ELUL, MY good friend, David Ashear, conveyed to me the urgency of having a book available on the topic of *Shmirat Einayim* — protecting one's eyes from seeing improper sights. He explained that the book must "speak to our generation and help them win this great spiritual test." We discussed the logistics and began to plan the writing of the book. From its inception, David has been the driving force behind this book and secured all the resources needed for its production. May Hashem bless him and his family for shepherding this book into existence.

Mrs. Charlotte Friedland is to be complimented for her superb editing of the book and fleshing out the journal segments at the end of each chapter.

Mrs. Yehudit Channen greatly enhanced the publication with her wise suggestions and excellent editorial skills.

My wife, Tzivia, gave me many good ideas and made every effort to encourage the project and bring it to fruition.

My sons, Dovid and Ben Zion Reuven, assisted in countless ways and offered many wise suggestions.

Rounding out the editing team was Rabbi Ariel Asa,

Marcia Sternberg, and Zev Breirer. Mrs. Eden Chachamtzedek is to be complimented for her book design and layout.

I am grateful to the board of directors of the Salant Foundation, who are dedicated to the vision of spreading Mussar study throughout the world. The members are: Jay Rodin and Manfred Leventhal (Co-Presidents), David Newman, Moe Rice, Mark Fisher, Gary Estersohn, Rabbi Benyamin Miller (New York), David Litwack, Mordecai Litwack (Washington), Avraham Litzman (Atlanta), Ivan Sacks (Dallas), Sheldon Gittleson, Simcha Yoel Brauser, Aaron Moses, David Goldis, Barry Reichenberg, Alan Zavodnick, Kobi Chuchran (Florida).

I express my heartfelt thanks to the Creator of the universe, the Holy One, may He be blessed, for bringing this holy project to my hands and helping me to complete the writing of this book.

Zvi Miller
Ramat Beit Shemesh, Israel

WINDOWS OF THE
SOUL

Introduction:
Why We Need
"Windows of the Soul"

Dedicated as a merit for our children, Ilana, Aaron, and Aryeh
May Hashem bless you with success, health, and happiness in
your pursuit of Torah, mitzvot, and good deeds!
Love, Aba and Ema (Avraham and Joyce Litzman)

THE IMAGE OF HASHEM

THE BEGINNING OF spirituality is the clear recognition of our good and holy souls — the very essence of our being. The more we become aware of our exquisite inner goodness, the happier and more fulfilled we will be. Additionally, we will strive to strengthen and preserve our personal and precious sanctity — the Image of Hashem — that illuminates our being. (Ohr HaTzafon, The Alter of Slabodka)

From the ancient days of our ancestors, Avraham, Yitzchak, and Yaacov, we — the Jewish People — have made every effort to protect our holy souls from negative influences that surround us on every side. Despite terrible challenges, we have survived as a great spiritual nation, intact and whole.

> When Shem and Yefet covered up their father's nakedness, they held a blanket and walked backwards so as not to see him. They could have walked towards him and kept their eyes lowered. Why did they feel it necessary to walk backwards?
>
> Since the *Image of Hashem is etched upon the human countenance*, simply exposing the face to improper sights is spiritually harmful! Therefore, they walked backwards to protect their holy souls. (The Alsheich)

AN ANCIENT STRATEGY THAT LIVES ON

BILAAM KNEW THAT immorality is the antithesis of Torah. Therefore, he suggested piercing the spiritual armor of

Jewish men by exploiting their natural inclinations. Pinchas, the holy Kohen, courageously stood up and quashed Bilaam's evil scheme.

Today, the forces of *tumah,* impurity, are using the same devious tactic that Bilaam employed. We face an onslaught of immodest clothing and behavior in the streets, at work, in every public place and even in our own homes. We are bombarded by images so destructive that many of our great rabbis have proclaimed that we are now surrounded by the worst level of *tumah* in history.

Every person who learns *Windows of the Soul* takes up the "spear of Pinchas" and acquires powerful tools to protect himself from the *tumah* that beckons from all sides.

WINDOWS OF THE SOUL: A THIRTY-DAY PROGRAM

OUR EYES HAVE been described as the windows of the soul. The book now in your hands presents a concise thirty-day program for controlling what we see. It incorporates the teachings of the Master of Mussar — Rabbi Yisrael Salanter, *zt"l* — as well as halachah rulings and practical advice to give you a solid strategy for success.

May Hashem inspire us with the wisdom to apply these principles; and bless our efforts to raise our level of spirituality individually and as a nation, so that we will merit the redemptive reunion of the *Shechinah* and all *Klal Yisrael.*

When that happens, we will see the joyful outcome predicted by the prophet (Zechariah 14:9): "Hashem will be King over the entire world — on that day Hashem will be One and His Name will be One."

The Goal:
Self-Mastery

THE TALMUD TELLS us that when Alexander the Great reached the gate of *Gan Eden*, he called out, "Open the gate for me!" To his chagrin, he was turned away with the response, "This is the gate to Hashem, only the righteous may enter."

Alexander retorted, "I am a king of great renown. Since you refuse to open the gate, at least give me something from *Gan Eden*."

They gave him an eyeball. When he weighed it, stacking all of his gold and silver on one side of the scale and the eyeball on the other, he was shocked to discover that the eyeball outweighed all of his wealth.

He asked the wise men for an explanation and they said, "This is the eyeball of a human being. The human eye is never satisfied with what it sees; it always wants more. Nothing in the world is enough, for a person will crave whatever he sees. In fact, his eyes are not satisfied until the day he dies and his eyes are covered with earth."

"Can this be true?" Alexander asked.

The wise men countered, "Cover the eye with a little earth. The true weight of the gold will reverse the scale immediately." (*Tamid* 32b)

Hashem denied Alexander access to *Gan Eden* because

of his greed and obsession with power. Bent on conquering the entire world, his desires were inflamed beyond all reason. When he demanded the reason for his rejection, he was given an eyeball, because the eye is the source of desire. Just as his desire was out of control, so too, the weight of the eyeball was completely out of proportion.

Heaven was hinting to him about the futility of chasing after earthly desires which can never be satisfied. But Alexander lacked the Torah wisdom to perceive this truth and could not see anything beyond his own ego and self-gratification. This mighty warrior conquered most of the world, yet he could not overpower his own eyes.

I want to control my eyes, but I feel that I haven't got the will-power. Is there a Torah formula that can help me?

You Can Count on Divine Assistance

MANY PEOPLE WOULD consider Alexander the epitome of strength. Undefeated in battle, he was one of the greatest military leaders in the history of the world. He was also a highly educated man, taught by Aristotle. Yet, he lacked both the strength and the wisdom to curb his insatiable eyes.

In contrast, the Mishnah (*Avot* 4:1) teaches, "Who is a man of strength? One who conquers his passions." Strength is defined as the mastery over one's desires. Our *Avot*, Avraham, Yitzchak, and Yaakov — were focused on spiritual pursuits and used their Torah knowledge to attain purity and closeness to Hashem. Unlike temporary world conquerors, they were true kings with eternal power because they mastered themselves. We, the People of Israel, have inherited their spiritual genes and dignified stature. The awareness of our intrinsic worthiness — and our royal lineage — inspires us with the confidence that we can rule over the lesser part of ourselves. The Torah gives us the wisdom to master our passions.

If the goal of self-discipline seems beyond you, it's important to know that you are not alone. There is a Torah formula that shows us how to attain Hashem's help. Specifically, our Sages teach us that if a person wants to cleanse himself spiritually, he will receive Divine assistance to succeed. The yearning for *taharah*, purity, burns in the heart of every Jew. Once we begin to strive for it, Hashem will help us gain control of our eyes. This control, in turn, will give us the key to control our thoughts and actions.

TODAY: *Know that if you sincerely want to achieve self-mastery, Hashem will surely help you.*

STEVE'S JOURNAL...

This is the first day of my journal. I've never done this before — writing down things that happen to me and what I think about on a daily basis — but I'm willing to try.

My best buddy, Dave, told me it's "essential" if you want to improve yourself.

And I do have a particular challenge I want to overcome. Sometimes, I'm distracted by immodest sights. I am a good Jew; but with all the visual challenges in the city, I didn't think there was a way that I could always control my eyes.

Dave and I work near each other in Manhattan, so we walk together from the train to our offices. The sights along the way are getting bolder and bolder. When I brought up this topic with Dave, I thought he would agree with me that there's nothing much I can do about it.

But he didn't agree. He said there's plenty I can do. That's not exactly what I expected to hear, but the more I thought about what he said, the more right he seemed. When I said, "I feel like I'm alone. Nobody can really help me," you should have heard him! He practically shrieked at me. He actually stopped walking and turned to face me.

"You can't think that way! Don't you know who you are? Your great-grandfathers are Avraham, Yitzchak and Yaakov. You've got the spiritual genes to overcome any challenge. Besides, you don't have to do it alone."

"You'll help?"

"Hashem will help. The Torah promises us that if we really aim to rid ourselves of bad habits Hashem will help us succeed. The more you want it, the more He'll help. You'll see."

"Do you think the Torah is talking about this kind of habit—something this personal, I mean?"

"Especially with 'this kind' of habit. Listen, that prohibition not to 'stray after your eyes,' is one of the six *mitzvot t'mediot*, one of the six *mitzvot* that we have to

31

keep in mind at all times, all day long.* First, you've got to commit to the idea of improving yourself, of course…"

"Okay, okay, I really want to try.'"

"Nice going. Now you have to start a notebook, some kind of journal so you can keep track of your progress."

When he said that, I was ready to get off right there. It sounded like too much work already. But I really do want to improve myself, to elevate my thoughts and really gain control over my eyes. I said I'd give it a try.

So here goes. I hope Dave knows what he's talking about.

---

*Bi'ur Halachah, Chapter 1

DAY

2

The Rambam Warns: Don't Rationalize!

Dedicated by Benhoor & Limor Hanasabzadeh as a Zechut for their children Elchanan, Itzchak Ariel, Avital, Ayelet and Bat-Sheva to grow up in Kedushah v'Taharah.

THE SOURCE OF the restriction of not looking at a woman if she is immodestly dressed is the Biblical verse, "Do not stray after your eyes." (*Bamidbar* 15:39)

What is so bad about admiring women?
Shouldn't I appreciate my wife?

The Torah's purpose is not to deny us the joy of a meaningful relationship with a woman. In fact, marriage is considered the ideal state of man. In creating Chava as the *ezer k'negdo*, the Divinely-appointed helper of Adam, Hashem confirms that "It is not good for man to be alone." This relationship is meant to help every individual live at the highest spiritual level he or she can reach. From this shared goal, children will be brought into the world who will continue as *Ovdei Hashem*, servants of G-d.

Rather, the purpose of the Torah's laws of *Shmirat Einayim* is to help us give our full love and attention to our wives. The awareness that your wife is the only woman permitted to you strengthens the unique and special bond of love between you.

Once we understand the benefits of the laws, we realize that they are not restrictions, but safeguards to enhance the quality of our lives. We cherish these Divine laws because they are the cornerstone of a successful marriage and the foundation for a healthy family.

Men, in general, have a strong natural desire for women. In addition to preserving our special relationship with our spouses, the Torah gives us guidelines so that these inclinations do not rule our lives. They save us from distraction, and even from destruction. If "destruction" seems like an exaggerated term in this context, consider the words of the Rambam.

Fully aware of the natural tendency of men to minimize the relevance of these laws, he writes:

> There are some transgressions for which a person is not motivated to repent because he considers them trivial and of no real consequence. Among them is the transgression of looking at women. A man who looks at a woman [feels he has done nothing wrong and] inwardly protests, "Did I have relations with her? Did I get close to her?" He doesn't realize that gazing at women who are forbidden to him is a transgression because it leads him to inappropriate conduct... (*Hilchot Teshuvah,* Chapter 4, Law 4)

THE MOST POWERFUL PREVENTATIVE

THE RAMBAM IS warning that promiscuity begins with gazing at women who are forbidden to you. Even though a man may rationalize that he is above such behavior, the Rambam informs him that self-control must start at the beginning. Controlling our eyes from looking at women is the most powerful preventative. *Like a loving parent who sets limits on his children for their own safety, the To-rah instructs us not to look at women for our own spiritual and physical well-being.*

Inadvertent Seeing

YOU MIGHT BE wondering: how can a man live in the world without seeing immodestly dressed women? Isn't it inevitable that every time he steps into any public area his eyes will take in everything?

The fact is that we are required to avoid looking at immodestly dressed women and images, and to develop an aversion to looking. As long as one follows these two stipulations, even if he inadvertently sees, he is not culpable. But after inadvertently seeing, he must turn his eyes away. If he continues looking or takes a second look, he commits the *aveirah* of "straying after his eyes."

TODAY: *Resolve to practice the laws of Shmirat Einayim for your own protection and to enhance your marriage.*

STEVE'S JOURNAL...

I made it a point to get to Mr. Lawrence's office early for our appointment. He's one of our most important clients—I couldn't let anything go wrong! But as soon as I walked up to the reception desk, I felt challenged. His secretary was not dressed appropriately for a business office. She smiled and said, "Mr. Lawrence is expecting you.

Let me show you to his office."

I was caught off guard, and I struggled to control my eyes as we walked down the long corridor. My mind was racing. How can I gain control? I had been told to focus my mind on holy thoughts, but they all flew out of my mind at that moment.

"Just a second," I said, as I bent down, pretending to fix my shoelace. Staring for a split-second at the floor, I recalled how the Rambam warned that big *aveirot* start as small, uncontrolled thoughts. That is a sobering thought. I kept that in mind as I continued walking.

By the time we reached the end of the hall, I felt that I had mastered a rough moment. I greeted Mr. Lawrence with a big smile and a firm handshake.

DAY

3

Commit to a
New Beginning

Dedicated by Joseph & Pouneh Hanasabzadeh as a
Zechut for their children Daniella, Binyamin Yoshiahu
and Yehudah to grow up in Kedushah v'Taharah.

3

IF WE HAVE not properly guarded our eyes in the past, we can change our behavior and Hashem will help us to improve our ways.

In fact, Hashem sent us an uplifting and encouraging message through the prophet Yechezkel: "Throw off all of your *aveirot* and make a new heart and a new spirit for yourselves." (Based on *Yechezkel* 18:30)

> *I feel burdened by my past conduct. It's hard for me to believe that Hashem will forgive me.*

Rabbenu Yonah offers this illuminating encouragement:

If a person has acted improperly and wants to take shelter beneath the "Wings of the *Shechinah*"… I will show him the way to proceed.

On the day that you lift your heart to return to Hashem, throw off all of your *aveirot* as if they never were. Consider yourself as a newborn child, having neither merit nor culpability. Today is the beginning of your actions. Today you will reflect on all of your ways… This outlook will facilitate your complete return to Hashem because you will be unburdened from the weight of all of your *aveirot*.

Do not be hindered by thoughts that hold you back from returning to Hashem. You might feel, "How can I have the nerve to return to Hashem, after I acted so inappropriately so many times? How can I come before Hashem? I feel embarrassed, like a thief who was caught in the act of stealing. … How can I observe His *mitzvot*?"

Do not allow these negative thoughts to enter your heart! These feelings of despair are the influence of the *yetzer hara.*

Rather, know that the arms of our Merciful Creator are always open to welcome those that return to Him. (*Yesod HaTeshuvah*)

Hashem releases us from the psychological barriers to repentance by urging us to throw off our misdeeds. In this way, He grants each one of us the opportunity to change our ways, regardless of our past conduct. He lets us renew ourselves and gives us a fresh start.

TODAY: *Throw off the burden of your aveirot and start over. Hashem gives everyone another chance!*

STEVE'S JOURNAL…

I've been thinking about what Dave said. He was so certain that Hashem would help me, and at the time, I believed him. But today, I almost lost my nerve and nearly abandoned my goal of winning the battle of the eyes.

Not that I haven't been momentarily successful. The

elevator in my office building is usually pretty crowded and, especially in the summer, this close proximity is a real challenge to a well-meaning Jew. Today, I stepped into the elevator and concentrated on keeping my eyes in check. It worked, and as I stepped out of the elevator, I felt pretty good about it!

But then another side of me—the cynical side—seemed to take over. "Sure you did it this time," an inner voice chided me, "but what about last week? You may as well give up now. You're fooling yourself."

I fought back. "Dave assured me that Hashem forgives the past. Old failures don't count," I told myself. To convince myself further, I pulled a paper out of my pocket on which I had written Rabbenu Yonah's powerful message about eliminating self-defeating guilt. Rereading it, I felt like Rabbenu Yonah had read my mind.

I needed to hear it again—to know without a doubt that Hashem is so loving and understanding that He will help me overcome fear, guilt, even past failures. Dave told me that Hashem will convert those failures into merits, because in battling them I connect to a deep reservoir of *kedushah*.

Imagine that! It takes real love—love beyond human comprehension—for Hashem to forgive and help anyone who wants to improve. But He does. Prophets and Sages have been telling us so for centuries.

I'm glad I decided to carry around that quote from Rabbenu Yonah. Today's setback actually led to bolstering my resolve. I'm not giving up!

DAY

4

Remember That You Are a Member of a Unique Nation

Dedicated by Benhoor & Joseph Hanasabzadeh
L'ilui Nishmat Yoshiahu Ben Elazar zt"l, Asher Ben Aba zt"l,
Yaakov ben Itzhak zt"l, Aba Ben Asher zt"l, Yosef ben Asher zt"l
and Ezra Ben Elazar zt"l.

4

"And Hashem spoke to Moshe, saying, Speak
to all the community of the Children of
Israel and say to them: You shall be holy,
for I, Hashem your G-d, am holy."

(Vayikra 19:2)

*How can a human being, who has a physical
body and earthly desires, become "holy"?*

AT MOUNT SINAI, Hashem gave the Torah to the entire Jewish Nation and conferred the status of *Kedushat Yisrael* upon us. This means that He implanted a unique and permanent holiness into every Jewish soul.

Whenever a person is tempted to act in a way that is against the Torah and he controls himself, he elevates himself spiritually and fulfills the *mitzvah* of "You shall be holy." Since his control is a fulfillment of this *mitzvah*, he is rewarded, just as Hashem rewards him for all the other *mitzvot* that he performs. He ascends to a higher spiritual level than he was on before.

THE HOLY COMMUNITY

NOW YOU MIGHT think that just because you withhold yourself from sinning, you aren't really "holy" and this verse does not refer to you. But it does. The verse says, "Speak to **all** the Children of Israel and say to them, "You shall be holy…" **The Torah is teaching us that holiness is not exclusively reserved for *tzaddikim*, but for any Jew who attempts to elevate himself.** *(Ohr HaChaim)*

This is an incredible concept! Control of our eyes is not just an inner battle between desire and restraint. We master ourselves countless times during the day and therefore, in Hashem's Eyes, we have the highest status — we are holy!

In fact, every time we succeed, we increase our own personal sanctity as well as that of the entire world. Once we understand this concept, we have the method and the motivation to gain control of our eyes. When we internalize the idea that we are holy in Hashem's Eyes, we feel happy with ourselves and we feel inspired to reach for higher levels in Torah and *mitzvot*.

TODAY: *Each time you control your eyes from looking at an improper sight, tell yourself, "I am a member of a holy nation."*

STEVE'S JOURNAL…

While waiting for the bus today, a woman came to the bus stop. Her clothing was immodest. My instant mental reaction was, "This is a spiritual test! Act now!" I casually moved to the other side while lowering my eyes so she would be out of my visual range.

A few weeks ago, I never would have believed that I could guard myself so effectively. But I've been doing some thinking about the "holiness" that Dave says is inborn in every Jew.

That word "holy" sounded so lofty when he first said it. I think of great rabbis and teachers as being holy, not regular people like me. But I was wrong. Dave explained that holy simply means being able to set yourself apart from the world-at-large, able to reach for spiritual goals. He showed me where the Torah says that every Jew can be holy. Even me.

"You don't know your own soul, Steve," he laughed. "You have what it takes to 'be holy' even if you don't think so."

So now I think of these challenging encounters as opportunities to gain spirituality, a chance to use the powers that Hashem gave me. Instead of shuddering when an improper sight crosses my path, a little bell goes off in my head, and my inner voice says, "Here's your chance."

DAY

5

Torah Study Is Your First Line of Defense

A VODAT HASHEM — Divine Service — is a general term that embraces a wide range and many levels of Torah observance. For our purposes, we are defining "Divine Service" as compliance with Torah Law (*Halachah*) and Torah Ethics (Mussar). In this light, Divine Service encompasses the fulfillment of the *mitzvot* (the positive commandments), and the avoidance of *aveirot* (the prohibitions).

Simply put, an observant Jew performs Divine Service by observing the Torah to the best of his or her ability.

I sincerely want to improve my Avodat Hashem by mastering my eyes. Where do I start?

YOUR HOLY SOUL

A PERSON'S REAL essence is his soul, which by definition is holy. The soul is entirely spiritual, but because it is attached to a physical body, its spiritual light becomes dimmed. The expression of that spirituality is through a person's good character traits and *mitzvot*. A *tzaddik* is often described as having a "shining countenance" because his soul is so developed that he is radiant. If we neglect our spiritual side, however, bodily forces gain the upper hand and base character traits, followed by *aveirot*, emerge.

"My son, give Me your heart and let your eyes observe My ways." (*Mishlei* 23:26) The Midrash explains that Hashem is saying, "If you give Me your heart and eyes, then you are My children." This means that control of your heart and eyes is a major criterion for being close to Hashem.

Viewing improper images creates a detrimental force which can easily overturn our spiritual equilibrium. It has the power to undo our entire spiritual foundation. How is that?

Your soul is a fiery element. Just as water extinguishes a blazing fire, the *tumah* of these images extinguishes our spiritual powers. Even worse, since the eyes are connected to the brain, the images that we see remain lodged within our mind, causing lingering ill effects.

Just as actual vision is impaired when the physical eye is injured, spiritual vision is impaired when the eyes are exposed to immodesty. This damage diminishes our ability to perceive the truth and to connect to Hashem.

FIRST STEP SOLUTION

THE FIRST LINE of defense for controlling our eyes and heart is Torah study. The Rambam explains that the heart only occupies itself with one thought at a time. If a man's heart is left to its own meanderings, it invariably gravitates towards unclean thoughts. However, if the heart is occupied with Torah, it will be filled with holy thoughts.

He concludes that Torah study is indispensable to gaining mastery over improper inclinations.

The positive thoughts stimulated by Torah study will empower us with the capability to serve Hashem.

TODAY: *Set up the first line of defense to mastering your eyes by dedicating daily time to Torah study.*

STEVE'S JOURNAL...

I knew there would be more to this than just keeping a journal. Yesterday, Dave advised me to buckle down on my Torah study. We're good friends, so he knows that I look over the *parshah* on Shabbat, but since I entered the working world, my Torah learning isn't as regular as it used to be."

But he was insistent. "Look," he said, "I know you're really trying to master your eyes, so it's logical to spend at least a little time each day studying Torah. Can't you find twenty minutes a day? C'mon, just twenty minutes."

Now how did he know that Rabbi Levy had announced that day that he would be starting a class right after *Shacharit*? Most of the men in our minyan are on their way to work, so he said he'd keep it short.

I think I should give it a try. Going to an early-morning Torah class will give me something worthwhile to think about all day—especially when those visual challenges come my way.

DAY

6

Mussar + Halachah = A Powerful Antidote

6

L ET'S NOW TURN towards the writings of Rabbi Yisrael Salanter, whose wise counsel will map out a means for mastering our eyes. Rabbi Salanter was the founder of the Mussar Movement, which in many ways revolutionized modern Jewish thought. In the classic work, *Ohr Yisrael* (the writings of Rabbi Salanter and his disciple, Rabbi Yitzchak Blazer), he wrote, "Without Mussar study, Avodat Hashem cannot be established" (Letter Three).

What does that mean? In a nutshell, Mussar is intended to achieve character refinement and illuminate one's personal spiritual growth. It is an exploration of our relationship with others, with our own self and with Hashem. With its sharp focus on elements of Torah that uplift and encourage, it has the strength to literally change your life. *Avodat Hashem* begins with a person who is inspired to improve himself and is aware of his potential to be closer to Hashem.

Rabbi Salanter speaks of the healing powers of Torah when you are facing a particular challenge. He assures you that not only can Torah reverse the negatives in your life; it can build an entirely new person. In *Igeret HaMussar*, he writes:

> *The way to utilize the healing powers of Torah is to continually study the laws relevant to the particular transgression…*

We know that transformation of human nature is generated by Torah study and the repeated practice of a desired good conduct or character trait. *This method of study causes a strong alteration within one's soul.* ...One's character will gradually change so that the transgression is naturally distant from him.

How can studying Torah law help me control strong impulses?

Rabbi Salanter uses the analogy of a physical disease. A person needs to relate to a spiritual malady in the same way he deals with a physical illness. The strength and dosage of the remedy is proportionate to the severity of the illness. The development of *Yirat Shamayim* (an acute awareness of Hashem's presence) and the study of the relevant laws is a primary remedy. As long as the *yetzer hara* is activated, *Yirat Shamayim* and the study of the appropriate laws must be increased. If a person does not use this primary remedy, then the general study of Torah will not have much influence over his *yetzer hara.* (*Ohr Yisrael, Igeret HaMussar*)

You may not have been aware that there are specific laws of *Shmirat Einayim*. It pays to find out about them, study them, and work on *Yirat Shamayim*, as outlined by Rabbi Salanter. The combination of Mussar study with the study of *halachah* yields a powerful tool for combating our physical desires. Learning what is forbidden and what is permitted will effectively guard you from seeing improper sights. If you sincerely and carefully study these laws, you are well on your way to a character transformation.

Even though it can be hard in the beginning, don't give up! The mores of modern society make this a very difficult test. But the combination of learning Mussar and studying the *halachot*, is so powerful that you will soon develop new habits that will stay with you forever.

TODAY: *Be encouraged by knowing that through Mussar and halachah study you have the means to control your eyes and change old habits.*

STEVE'S JOURNAL...

I had to pay a *shiva* call today, and to tell you the truth, I really dreaded it. I knew that Joe had been particularly close to his father and that losing him would be a terrible blow. He has two brothers and a sister, too, and I expected the entire household to be inconsolable.

As I walked into the room, I was truly surprised. Joe's siblings, as I predicted, were having a tough time. But Joe, though obviously mournful, seemed calm and meditative. You could see that he had some kind of inner strength the others lacked. He noticed my reaction, and he turned to me, asking why I seemed puzzled. At the risk of being rude, I told him.

"Joe, I know how sad you must feel, yet you seem to be taking it in stride—to be honest, better than I expected you to." He smiled faintly. "What's the secret?" I blurted. He thought for a moment.

"Well, for the past ten years, Dad and I studied Mussar together. We had a regular *chavrutah* once a week. At first, it's imperceptible, but eventually Mussar changes your whole perspective. I feel that I'm in touch with a level of reality that's very comforting. It's kind of hard to explain, but it's very real to me."

"Mussar did that?"

"That and more. It's not only helping me through this experience, it has put me in touch with real joy, too. I can honestly say it's helped me deal with tough challenges as well."

"Your father was very wise to teach you all that."

"He saw it as preparing me for life. We learned *halachah* together too. He let me choose the topic, depending on what I needed to learn at the time."

What a legacy! As I left, I couldn't help thinking that Joe's father had given him a priceless gift.

Know the Laws of
Shmirat Einayim

Donated by Alan Mizrachi in memory of:
Hacham Baruch Refael Ben-Haim ben Miriam zt"l,
Menachem ben Simcha, Selma bat Sarah,
Abraham Sion ben Naava.

$$\boxed{7}$$

IN RECENT YEARS, many of us have become more aware of Torah laws governing *Shmirat HaLashon*, and now we are careful about what we say and what we hear. When we were first introduced to the laws of *Shmirat HaLashon*, we might have felt overwhelmed. But with study and practice, keeping these laws became easier.

In the same way, when we first hear the laws of *Shmirat Einayim* we may think, "This is impossible! There's no way I can be this careful." But as we study, we understand the wisdom of these laws and the more motivated we become.

The Four Primary Laws of Looking at and Thinking about Women

Below is a summary of relevant rulings. Familiarize yourself with these laws, and you will have a ready and practical guide to live by:*

(1) It is forbidden to look at a woman if she is dressed immodestly. (There are different laws regarding one's wife.)

(2) a. If you know of an area where immodestly dressed

Shulchan Aruch Even HaEzer, Chapter 21, Law 1.

women are present, it is forbidden to enter this area. An alternative route must be taken.

b. If there is no alternative route, or the alternative route is impractical or costly, you are permitted to pass through the area providing you make every reasonable effort to avoid seeing the immodest sights.

(3) It is forbidden to have thoughts of desire for any woman. (There are different laws regarding one's wife.)

(4) It is forbidden to derive pleasure from looking at the beauty of a woman, even if she is modestly dressed. (There are different laws regarding one's wife.)

Clearly, these laws are not easy to apply in situations where women cannot be avoided, such as a work setting. The upcoming segments will deal with specific advice and techniques regarding various scenarios.

Does the Torah think men are angels?
How can any man realistically fulfill these laws?

It's very true that controlling your eyes is a tremendous challenge. The Torah does not expect that we will gain total control instantaneously. Changing ourselves takes study and the persistent practice of new behavior — until it becomes second nature. With sincere motivation, studying this guidebook and applying its principles, eventually you will win the "battle of the eyes."

TODAY: *Know that like every law in the Torah, the laws of Shmirat Einayim were designed for real people, just like you. Resolve to review these laws periodically in order to strengthen your observance of them.*

STEVE'S JOURNAL...

Dave and I finally got serious about learning the *halachot* of *Shmirat Einayim*. We reasoned that you can't decide to just "be careful" in this area any more than you can just "be careful" about *kashrut*. You have to know the laws. So last night he came over to my house and we reviewed and discussed these four basic laws.

At first, these laws seemed overwhelming, but I can handle them knowing that we don't have to change overnight. Little by little, I'll try to integrate them into my life.

So we started to learn. I committed the four basic rules to memory.

Wouldn't you know, I had a challenging test today. This morning, I walked into the conference room for a business meeting. Three of the six people in the room were women, and two of them were dressed immodestly. The laws were fresh in my mind, so I was immediately conscious of being careful where I looked. Knowing the specific guidelines made a real difference. I felt I was in control.

DAY

8

We Are Never "Immune" to Immodesty

"When B'nai Yisrael went down to Egypt, they behaved with modesty — each person living in his own tent, as the verse says (Shemot 1:1): 'Each man and his household came.' Reuven did not look at Shimon's wife, nor did Shimon look at Reuven's wife. Rather, each man lived modestly within his own tent. Even when the population of men numbered 600,000 in the desert, not one man placed the opening of his tent opposite the opening of his friend's tent."

(*Yalkut Shimoni, Balak*)

In ancient days, life was different and people were different too. In the modern world, we are so used to seeing women in public that we have grown somewhat "immune" to them. So shouldn't these laws and teachings be modified?

YES, TIMES HAVE changed, and there are some leniencies in the fine details of some of these laws. Please consult your rabbi for specific questions and rulings. The four laws that we learned in Day 7, however, are *d'Oraitah, direct Torah prohibitions,* and immutable.

A standard rationale offered by those who are lax in *Shmirat Einayim* is the idea that we've grown so used to seeing women immodestly dressed in public that it barely affects us anymore.

One of the greatest *Ba'alei Mussar* was Rabbi Eliyahu Lopian, who taught Torah for over seventy years in Europe and *Eretz Yisrael*. One of his students was invited to a wedding where the laws of modesty would not be observed. He asked Rabbi Lopian if he could go to the wedding. When asked what he would do about the lack of *tzniut*, the student told him that the sight of immodest women does not affect him. Without another word, Rabbi Lopian reached for a book of *Tehillim* and started praying. "Rabbi, what are you doing?" asked the student.

His teacher responded, "I am 86 years old and blind in one eye, and I am still affected by human nature. You are young and in the prime of life. If you are not affected by immodest sights, then perhaps you're sick. I am saying *Tehillim* for your recovery!"

There are others who feel that they are somehow above the law. King Solomon was the wisest of men. He knew that the Torah limits how many wives a king is permitted to marry. Yet he reasoned that the Torah's restriction is for an average king. Since he was so wise, he thought that the Torah's law did not apply to him. Far exceeding the maximum number permitted, he eventually had "700 wives, princesses, and 300 concubines…" The result was that, "When he was old, his wives turned his heart away."

Think of it! King Solomon, the tzaddik who built the Beit HaMikdash, was the son of King David. He was the Gadol HaDor and the wisest man who ever lived. Imbued with ruach hakodesh, he composed the holy books of Shir HaShirim, Mishlei, and Kohellet. Despite his unfathomable greatness, he was not immune to being influenced by an aspect of desire.

None of us are anywhere near his level. How much more so should we take every precaution to fulfill these halachot! Even if we don't fully understand the relevancy of the laws, as Torah Jews we must observe them.

TODAY: *Defer to the wisdom of the Torah regarding the laws of Shmirat Einayim. They are relevant to every generation and every circumstance.*

STEVE'S JOURNAL...

The invitation to Brett and Cindy's wedding came the other day. Neither one is an observant Jew, and their families know nothing about *tzniut*. Now that I've made a commitment to control my eyes, my first reaction was "I can't go!"

But I see Brett at the office every day and he seems really anxious for me to be there. "Don't worry, Steve," he keeps urging me, "I'll order kosher food for you." How could he understand if I tell him there'll be more there that's not kosher besides the food?

If it were anybody else, I would simply send a nice gift and explain that I will not be able to attend. Usually, that's acceptable (especially if it's a really nice gift!), and I don't have to compromise my Torah standards.

But in this case, I'll have to show up, at least for part of the time. I told Brett that he can count on me to be there for the ceremony, but right after the ceremony, I'll have to be on my way. "And you'll save on that kosher meal," I kidded him.

I've been told that even if they wear an immodest dress for the reception, some women cover up for the "religious" part of the wedding. If I'm lucky, that will be the case. If not, I'll have to put into action everything I've learned about *Shmirat Einayim*. In any case, I'll leave just as soon as I can.

DAY 9

Listen to Your Soul

In tribute to David Ashear who had the foresight and courage
to address an area of great spiritual importance.

Dr. & Mrs. Jack Cohen

9

RABBI YISRAEL SALANTER commented on the sophisticated mechanism in our minds that rationalizes wrongdoing. We actually convince ourselves that we are blameless. He writes:

> Physical desires urge a man to label what is impure as 'Pure!' But when he comes for his final judgment before Hashem, his improper indulgences will be rightfully called 'Impure!' and he will be recompensed accordingly. (*Ohr Yisrael*, Letter Four)

Does desire really distort reason?
We can't really fool ourselves, can we?

Desire in our generation is like a fire out of control, a force of great strength and danger. Like a salesman with an "I won't take no for an answer" attitude, it is relentless in its effort to sell us a slick catalogue of tantalizing goodies. The lofty soul objects, saying, "This is an *aveirah!*"

Shouldn't the objection of the intelligent and sensitive soul stop the momentum of desire? Logically, yes. Yet we often act in ways that are against our better judgment. Think about the abuse of alcohol, cigarettes, food, and money. Consider the consequences of anger, jealousy, and greed. How can we explain the fact that people often fail to control themselves, even when they know they should?

Rabbi Salanter observed, "The distance between the mind and the heart is as far as the distance from the earth to the heavens." In other words, what we **know** is not necessarily what we **feel**, nor does it govern our behavior. Mussar teaches that desire silences the protestations of the soul by intensifying until it extinguishes all objections.

In other words, passion blinds a person from thinking rationally. It is so powerful that it can short-circuit our own value system, to the point that we deem what is clearly "*impure* as *pure*." In our right mind, we would have seen something as wrong and degrading. But once desire is inflamed, we might end up doing something that we ourselves will later consider inappropriate and immoral.

The wisdom of Mussar helps us understand what is taking place so we can protect ourselves. Once you comprehend this mechanism, that your desire will try to stifle your soul, you have the means to control your eyes. With this important information, you are empowered to **listen to your intellect**. Now you have a chance to win!

TODAY: *Remember that desire will intensify in order to drown out the voice of reason. Understand that and listen closely to your soul.*

STEVE'S JOURNAL...

I passed Larry's cubicle again today. Ever since he came to work in our office, he's been a problem. His computer screen often has improper images and they're visible to whoever happens to be passing by.

Before I was really conscious of *Shmirat Einayim*, I used to rationalize that it was none of my business. But it is my business. I really feel — no, I know — that he's polluting the spiritual atmosphere. He's making it hard for me to work with him. I even got up the nerve to talk to my boss about it. He just chuckled and said, "Boys will be boys."

So I'm on my own, and I need a strategy. I decided that from now on, I'll go out of my way not to go down that corridor. If I do have to pass him, I'll make it a point to look the other way. And I discovered that most of the time I can work with him using email or the phone. If we have to meet, I suggest that he come to my desk, or meet me in the conference room.

Dave and I learned Rabbi Salanter's terrific insight that passion tries to justify everything by actually drowning out reason. I think Larry is a perfect example of its power. Just knowing that this is a battle between my soul and my desires helps me keep my head on straight!

DAY

10

Maintain a Balanced Approach: Treat Women with Respect

L'ilui Nishmat Mr. Jack Gemal
from Martin, Alice, Jack, Ike, Jean, and Adam Gemal.

"Common courtesy precedes Torah."
(Vayikra Rabbah 9:3)

**Couldn't not looking at a woman
be construed as rudeness?**

NATURALLY, EVERY SITUATION requires tact and common sense. The law does not expect us to treat modestly dressed women as if they do not exist. We are expected to develop a balance between controlling our eyes and treating women respectfully.

Rabbi Simcha Zissel Ziv, one of the foremost proponents of Mussar, entered a restaurant accompanied by a colleague. The owner of the restaurant was delighted that two great rabbis had come to eat in her restaurant. She prepared a lavish meal and served them herself with respect and joy.

During the course of the meal, in her excitement over hosting such important guests, she told them about her special recipes and the running of her business. Rabbi Simcha Zissel listened attentively, asking questions and responding to her answers. The other rabbi buried his head in a book and paid no attention to the woman's conversation.

When the rabbis were ready to pay for the meal, she refused to accept their money. "Should I lose the merit of this *mitzvah*," she exclaimed, "for a few coins?"

Afterwards, Rabbi Simcha Zissel turned to his friend and said, "Aren't you concerned that you ate and drank without paying?"

"What do you mean?" his companion replied, "She refused any payment!"

"You're right," said Rabbi Simcha Zissel, "She didn't want any money. But she wanted very much to speak with us and you completely ignored her. You took her meal without giving her any compensation."

Undoubtedly, Rabbi Simcha Zissel kept his eyes and thoughts properly trained. Yet out of consideration for his hostess, he maintained the *halachot* of guarding his eyes without compromising the Torah axiom to show appreciation to others. We learn from his example that each situation requires good judgment. When women are dressed modestly, we can observe the Torah's laws, and at the same time give them attention and respect.

TODAY: *Use a balanced approach — understand that the laws of Shmirat Einayim do not allow you to deny women respect and consideration.*

STEVE'S JOURNAL...

I have to admit that I was a little confused. I was invited to *Sheva Brachot* at the Cohen's house tonight, and I wasn't sure of "Torah etiquette." Should I thank the hostess or is it better not to look at her or say anything?

So I called my number one authority, Dave. "I've been invited too," he answered. "Meet me at 7:30 in front of the Cohens' house."

When we met, Dave told me it's all a question of balance. After all, the Torah wants you to be a "*mensch*." "Just follow me," he instructed, "and do what I do."

We went inside. Mrs. Cohen was at the door and Dave cordially greeted her. I thanked her for inviting me and followed him to the table. It was a great *Sheva Brachot*. The food was magnificent, the speeches were short, and the newlyweds looked really happy.

When the *kallah*'s friends came in, Dave gave me a little under-the-table kick and pointedly looked down at his plate. He didn't have to: I was already studying the silverware.

When it was over, Dave and I thanked Mrs. Cohen for the terrific meal she had served. She really glowed. Putting together a *Sheva Brachot* like that takes a lot of hard work, and I think she was glad that we appreciated it.

DAY

11

Develop Your Awareness of Hashem

Donated by Alan Mizrachi
in honor of Morris & Ben Mizrachi and Joyce Harary.

J UST AS A security guard will deter a thief from robbing a store, the awareness that you are in G-d's presence will empower you with the ability to control your eyes. Without *Yirat Shamayim*, genuine awareness of Hashem, it is impossible to overcome desire.

Awareness of Hashem is hard to sustain in today's culture. What tools can I utilize to help me develop and maintain it?

King Solomon explained that *Yirat Shamayim* is the sole antidote for our *yetzer hara* (*Kohellet* 11:9). We define *Yirat Shamayim* as the awareness that:

(1) Hashem sees our actions and knows our thoughts.
(2) Hashem judges all of our deeds and metes out the consequences.

The spiritual reward and punishment that the soul experiences in the World to Come is infinitely greater than the physical pleasure and pain of this world.

HOW TO DEVELOP *YIRAT SHAMAYIM*

IN *OHR YISRAEL,* Rabbi Salanter confirms that, "*Yirat Shamayim* rules over everything. It has the power to curb desire and keep it in check." (Letter Four)

How can you access this powerful tool? The most effective way is through the daily study of Mussar. Some of the classical Mussar texts are:

❖ *Mesilat Yesharim* (The Path of the Just)
❖ *Orchot Tzaddikim* (The Ways of the Righteous)
❖ *Chovot HaLevavot* (Duties of the Heart)
❖ *Menorat HaMaor* (by Rabbi Yitzchak Abuhav)
❖ *Pirkei Avot* (Ethics of the Fathers)
❖ *Mishlei* (Proverbs)
❖ *Kohellet* (Ecclesiastes)

Several works that are more contemporary are relevant and enlightening as well. A few of them are:

❖ *Ohr Yisrael*
❖ *Michtav Me'Eliyahu* (Strive for Truth)
❖ *Ahavat Chesed* (Chofetz Chaim)
❖ *Ohr Gedalyahu*
❖ *Netivot Shalom*

Many works of Mussar have been translated into English, but none should be just read through quickly. It's best to study these works methodically with a mentor or a *chavruta*. If that is not possible, self-study is a workable option.

In *Maggid Mesharim*, Rabbi Yosef Caro, author of the *Shulchan Aruch*, records Torah teachings and secrets that were revealed to him by an angel. The angel instructed him, "Read one section from *Chovot HaLevavot* every day in order to humble the *yetzer hara*." If Rav Yosef Caro, who was a pure and holy *tzaddik,* was told to learn Mussar every day, is there any question that we need it even more?

In fact, the Rosh, the Tur, the Arizal, the Vilna Gaon and the *Mishnah Berurah* (chapters 1 and 603) ruled that every person should study Mussar every day. This is because, over time, continuous Mussar study instills the awareness that Hashem sees our actions and knows our thoughts. **This is the primary and indispensable weapon to gain self-mastery.** Once *Yirat Shamayim* is a reality to you, a force will be at your disposal that can effectively overcome desires.

MUSSAR STUDY PLAN

Guidelines
   (1) The key to success in Mussar is incremental steps.

   (2) Devote about 20 minutes a day to Mussar study.

   (3) Absorb the concepts at your own pace.

Method
   (1) Select a Mussar book.

   (2) Schedule a daily time for Mussar study.

   (3) Read it aloud so that it penetrates your heart.

   (4) Even if you don't sense any immediate change — persevere! With time, you will be transformed and elevated.

Internalize

(1) Highlight key ideas.

(2) Write these ideas on an index card.

(3) Carry the card with you.

(4) Review the ideas a few times a day.

(5) Know that Mussar is healing your soul.

TODAY: *Make a commitment to study Mussar each day for about twenty minutes.*

STEVE'S JOURNAL...

After my visit to Joe's *shiva*, I began to consider learning Mussar. Dave, of course, thought it was a great idea, and before I could stop him, he was pulling Mussar books off his bookshelves. "Here, take a look at these," he said, as he piled them up in front of me. "Every author has his own approach, but they all lead to greater awareness of Hashem. Where do you want to start?"

I balked. To tell the truth, I've always had a negative concept of "Mussar." There used to be a guy in our shul who rebuffed reprimands by defensively raising his hand and retorting, "Don't give me any Mussar!" So I always associated it with being scolded. Dave said that's not it at all!

"It's all about Hashem and us," he said gently. "It's about His love for us and why He gave us the laws we keep." So I had a second confession to make.

"Dave, forgive me if this sounds childish, but my

understanding is that G-d is a strict King, Whose main approach is punishment."

Dave slapped his forehead. "That's not only childish, it's not Jewish!" he groaned. "Of course, our obligations to Him are basic and we must remember He's watching us. But that's because He loves us."

Then Dave pointed out something incredible that he had learned in *Netivot Shalom*. When Hashem decided to take the Jewish People out of Egypt, he told Moshe to go to Pharaoh and tell him to release them: tell him they are "*B'ni bechori Yisrael* –Israel, My first-born [most beloved] son." Now at that point, we were at the 49th level of *tumah*! We were wallowing in practically the lowest level of depravity—yet Hashem called us His most beloved! And it's still true today. Every Jew has His unconditional love.

He was on a roll. "Don't we owe Him a commitment to follow His laws? That's where *Yirat Shamayim* comes in, Steve. It's the best weapon against giving in to temptation." That convinced me. I need to develop the kind of *Yirat Shamayim* that could stop me in my tracks. He said we should start learning Mussar for twenty minutes a day.

"Only twenty minutes?" I asked. "Can that really help?"

"You'd be surprised."

DAY

12

Create Your Own Spiritual Log

Dedicated by Eli Kairey:
In honor of my wife Marjorie,
by her husband and children.

12

WHEN THE JEWISH People were slaves in Egypt, Pharaoh was concerned that they would rebel and overthrow his rule. In order to prevent them from organizing a rebellion, he saw to it that they labored under a heavy and continuous workload. When Moshe and Aharon asked him to let the nation leave to worship their G-d, Pharoah interpreted their request as the first stage of revolt and responded, "Intensify their burdens!" *(Shemot* 5:9) They must not have a spare minute to devise a strategy.

Just as Pharaoh denied the Jews time for action, the fast pace of modern life gives us little time to reflect on our conduct. Even if we have learned the laws of *Shmirat Einayim*, we may have grown lax about them and not noticed how susceptible we are to improper sights.

Increasing our awareness of Hashem so we can effectively control our behavior requires conscientious vigilance. We must first be fully aware of our own actions, and this requires taking the time to think. The Talmud tells us that, **"A person who contemplates his path in this world will merit seeing the deliverance of Hashem."** (*Moed Katan* 5a)

That sounds like a good thing to do, but truthfully, I'm too busy to take the time.

Setting aside time daily for "spiritual accounting," is one of the most effective ways to review your behavior. In just a few minutes each day, you create a sense of accountability and heighten your awareness. Your "account" is strictly your own business. It is personal and should be kept private so you can accurately record questionable behavior without feeling embarrassed by other readers.

First, review the basic principles of *Shmirat Einayim*. Next, review your day to see your strong points and weak points. This is a highly effective way to strengthen your best traits and behavior and uproot *aveirot*.

For some people, a mental checklist at the end of each day works well. Many people benefit even more by keeping a small chart handy. In this way, you can view your progress over time.

On the next page is a sample chart for your spiritual log. Of course, you can create your own chart to reflect your own goals.

Place a "check" for times you were successful in controlling your eyes; place a "minus sign" when you did not exercise control.

SAMPLE CHART	SUN	MON	TUES	WED	THURS	FRI	AFTER SHABBAT
I controlled my eyes from seeing improper sights.							
I took an alternative route when possible.							
When I had to take a route where immodest sights are found, I still managed to control my eyes.							
Whenever I controlled my eyes, I remembered that I am part of a holy nation.							
I cut off improper thoughts.							
I reviewed the four laws learned on Day 7.							

TODAY: *Take a few minutes in the evening
to review your conduct of that day.*

STEVE'S JOURNAL...

At first, I was skeptical about keeping a written accounting on my effort to take control of my eyes. But even though it seemed excessive, I had to admit that I don't remember everything that transpires during the course of the day, and I tend to "forget" uncomfortable failings. So I decided to try it. I was a little nervous that it might be found by someone, so I devised abbreviations for each of the categories and tucked it away out of sight.

A fascinating pattern emerged when I reviewed last week's log. Until I saw it in black and white, I hadn't realized that I don't usually seek out alternative routes to problematic streets on my way to work. I just barrel through, trying not to look. But reading my log, I realized that I should be choosing better routes in the first place.

It's a funny thing. My wife, Sara, watches her weight by keeping track of what she eats and writing it down at the end of the day. She says it helps keep her "honest." It also makes her really aware of what she's consuming; I've seen her pull her hand back from that extra dessert knowing she will have to "report" it. I guess you could say I'm doing the same thing—watching what my eyes consume. Keeping track is just a device, but it's a clever one, and it seems to work for both of us.

DAY

13

Know the Guidelines for Unavoidable Situations

Dedicated by an anonymous sponsor.

THE DARKNESS OF night causes two types of visual misjudgment. In *Mesilat Yesharim* (chapter 3), the Ramchal explains that when it is dark:

(1) We cannot see a stumbling block in our path.

(2) We see something and imagine it to be something else. For instance, we see a tree and imagine it to be a man.

Corresponding to these forms of physical visual impairment, we are prone to two types of misperceptions:

(1) We fail to realize that a certain behavior conflicts with *Halachah*.

(2) We rationalize doing an *aveirah* by insisting that it is not an *aveirah*. We may even imagine it to be a *mitzvah*.

For example, even though we know we're prohibited from looking at a woman who is dressed immodestly, we may think that the female teller in the bank is excluded. After all, if we close our eyes, how can we conduct our business? So we decide that the prohibition does not apply in this case, or that it's even a *mitzvah* to look at her because it's necessary.

In today's world, it's unrealistic to avoid immodestly dressed women. What can I do in a situation that is unavoidable?

Yes, avoiding areas where women are immodestly dressed is a great challenge. As we learned on Day 7, *Halachah* stipulates that if there is an alternative route, you must take it. Yet, if there is no other reasonable alternative route, you are permitted to walk past immodestly dressed women if you follow these guidelines:

(1) Lower your gaze or partially close your eyes.*

(2) Ensure that they will not be in your view for a long time.

(3) If a man knows that he *cannot avoid* looking at them, he cannot go into that area.

Use strategies to keep your mind focused. For instance, as you enter the area, listen to a *shiur* on a portable device or call someone on your cell phone. Be prepared to turn your eyes away or close them as needed.

TODAY: *If you must be in an area of immodestly dressed women, keep your eyes lowered and distract yourself with something worthwhile.*

---

* *Bava Batra* 57b, see the Rashbam ad. loc.

STEVE'S JOURNAL...

As Dave and I were discussing the laws of *Shmirat Einayim*, it seemed to me that some of them were antiquated, considering the society around us. "Get real!" I told him, "This isn't the ancient Middle East, where women walk around with veils over their faces." He stared at me calmly.

"Steve, you know perfectly well that the Torah was written for all places and all times. It doesn't matter if you happen to be in Babylon or in Burbank."

"Well, I happen to be in midtown New York! And you know as well as I do what the challenges are around here. It's very nice to say 'find an alternate route.' There is no alternate route! One block is as bad as the other."

"Ok, there's a way to deal with that too. If you have no choice at all, lower your gaze."

"My what? Lower my what?"

"Your gaze, the angle of your vision. Focus more on the ground than on what's above it."

"I'll bump into something."

"No you won't. Tomorrow I'll show you how to do it; with just a little practice, it'll be second nature."

So tomorrow Dave is giving me" lower-your-gaze lessons," showing me how to use my eyes and feet to get where I need to go without breaking the *Shmirat Einayim* rules. I hope it's not like learning to swim. I was never good at that.

DAY

14

Prepare for the Unexpected

"**W**HEN AN ARMY plans a war, the generals design a strategy. They consider every detail and prepare for every scenario. But when the war is actually fought, there are always unforeseen events and situations that will come into play. So generals retain flexibility and prepare a backup plan in order to adjust the strategy as the war unfolds." (*Ohr Yisrael,* Letter 19)

Whenever we plan to battle the *yetzer hara* regarding our eyes, we have to remember that this plan is only an approximation. When we go out in public, we have to expect the unexpected.

The Vilna Gaon would review the second chapter in *Mesilat Yesharim,* which talks about "watchfulness," thirteen times before going out into the street. We are not on that level; but his example is an indication of how careful we have to be when entering a visual danger zone.

That all makes sense, but how can you prepare for what you don't expect?

The fact is that visual challenges are not really that unexpected. You can pretty much bet on the fact that somewhere along your route there will be individuals or images that are off limits. Once you leave the privacy of your home, you will be confronted by countless images. Since the intention of most of these images is to catch the eye, they are positioned at eye-level. Unrestrained, your eyes scan a wide area, dart up and down, back and forth, and react to everything they see. The more stimulating the image, the more your eyes will be attracted to it.

Your eye does not naturally lower its gaze below eye-level. **You have to make a conscious effort to lower your gaze.** This basic strategy is easy and attainable; and it doesn't mean staring at your shoes and bumping into street poles, or poking along looking strange!

With your eyes slightly lowered, just look straight in the direction you are walking. Your eyes will take in an area of about five to ten feet of your pathway. In the next chapter, you will learn how to train your eyes to do this. Although lowering your gaze is a highly effective strategy, it's not foolproof, so you will also need the other strategies outlined in the coming chapters.

TODAY: *Make a conscious effort to keep your gaze below eye-level when you are in a public place.*

STEVE'S JOURNAL...

Thankfully, learning to lower my focus was easier than learning to swim. I decided to try out my new skill on the way to work today. When I got off the train, I looked down a bit as I walked the streets to my office. At first, it felt unnatural and I thought people might say to me, 'Hey, fella, look where you're going!"

You know New Yorkers. I thought somebody might even ask me why I'm looking down. But nobody noticed. I started to feel more confident about it, and I noted that the majority of "routine" sights fell from my view. I made adjustments as I went along, finding it easier than I thought it would be.

You can't imagine how effective this is until you try it.

DAY

15

Practice Lowering Your Eye Level

*Dedicated by Mr. and Mrs. Alan Safdeye,
L'ilui Nishmat Yosef ben Salcha and Daniel ben Gilsom
and Avraham ben Sara.*

SINCE KEEPING YOUR eyes lowered is not the norm, you need to accustom yourself to this new focus. The best way to change an old habit is to consciously practice a new behavior. Over time, the new pattern of behavior will become second nature.

Changing my focus seems to be unnatural. Show me how I can train my eyes to avoid normal eye-level.

Here is an exercise that is designed to help you re-adjust the level of your gaze. Just as an army practices maneuvers before going into battle, we recommend practicing this exercise when you have a few spare moments.

FOCUSED VISION

(1) Choose a quiet area in your home or yard and designate a twenty-foot length as a practice path.

(2) Lower your gaze so that it takes in about five to ten feet of the path.

(3) Begin walking, and keep your eyes focused on the five feet length, moving your eyes a little further down the path as you walk.

(4) Turn around and repeat the exercise, returning to the starting point.

(5) Do this exercise every day for one week.

When you have the opportunity, close your eyes for a few minutes when you travel on a bus or train. Notice that you can experience the sounds and conversations around you without seeing them. (You might even try this at home, but first inform your family that you are doing an experiment and will close your eyes for a few moments.) This experience will help you realize that you can fully participate in life without seeing every detail occurring around you. Just knowing that fact will help you overcome your natural curiosity, downplaying the need to see everything going on. In this way, lowering your gaze as you walk down the street will not make you feel that you might miss something important.

TODAY: *Begin practicing this exercise, keeping in mind that it is part of your new commitment to achieve control over your eyes.*

STEVE'S JOURNAL...

As usual, I got off the train in midtown today and assessed the *Shmirat Einayim* situation. It's become a pretty solid mental habit to consciously stop and think before I go any further. I already know that no matter what route I choose to the office, there are going to be challenges along the way.

So today, I tried what I call my "Change Focus Mode." My eyes sort of locked into a lowered position, not looking at the ground, but focusing on just the five to ten feet ahead of me. "This is a war," I kept telling myself, "you worked on this maneuver, now do it!"

I walked just the way I had practiced in my backyard, and it worked! Somehow, I didn't feel the need to scan left and right, nor to take in all the alluring city sights. Before I knew it, I had reached my office building.

Victory!

DAY

16

Take One Day
at a Time

*"Routine and experience are the keys
to control in every matter."*

(*Ohr Yisrael,* Letter Four)

---

*"The keys to control" are exactly what I need! What do routine
and experience have to do with controlling my eyes?*

RABBI SALANTER USED the word "routine" quite in-
tentionally, for self-improvement does not happen
overnight. Character refinement is a process that takes
time. Develop a routine practice of guarding your eyes.
By making it a habit, you will eventually train your eyes
to avoid looking at improper images.

The slowness of your progress may frustrate you. Remember that just as you cannot detect the movement of
the hour hand on a clock unless you look at it intermit-
tently, it's hard to detect character transformation as it is
taking place.

Let's review the well-known story of Rabbi Akiva, who
began studying Torah at age forty, and felt little progress.
One day, he sat down near a spring and noticed a rock
with a hole that had been made by the dripping water. He
saw a wonderful message in this occurrence: "If water,

which is soft, can carve a rock, which is hard — then surely the Torah, which is so strong, can penetrate my heart which is only flesh and blood." (*Avot D'Rebbi Natan,* chapter 6)

This insight — that there is undetectable, but certain change — inspired Rabbi Akiva to rededicate himself to Torah. He understood that every word he learned infused him with spiritual health, life, and holiness. This awareness propelled him to become one of the greatest of our Sages.

The other key is experience. In your battle to overcome the curiosity of your eyes, there will be slip-ups and mistakes along the way. Unexpected images or challenging situations may catch you off-guard.

Even if you have the strongest dedication to self-improvement, it's critical to accept the fact that mistakes are part of the learning process. We need to learn the pitfalls in order to avoid them. The Talmud expresses this truth: "A person can only learn after he has erred." (*Gittin* 43a)

The realization that mastery over your eyes takes time and experience is very important for two reasons: first, to avoid the unrealistic expectation of instant change; and secondly, to understand that without occasional mistakes, we cannot really grasp the lesson.

Considering the tendency of human nature to be attracted to improper images, it is virtually impossible for a person to gain instant control of his eyes. If you react with guilt and despair every time you fall short, you will never learn from your error. But if you can identify the exact mistake, you will eventually learn not to repeat it.

TODAY: *Be patient with yourself! Take a look at the mistakes you've made, so you will be alert to these specific challenges in the future.*

STEVE'S JOURNAL...

Dave promised to watch his kids today while his wife went shopping, so I went over to his place to help him. His year-old baby, Linda, is learning to walk. I watched her for a while. She's still unsteady on her feet, but it was amazing to see how hard she tries. She takes a couple of steps, and then flops right down. It doesn't bother her a bit. She just gets right up and starts over, again and again.

Of course, we were patient with her. It wasn't her fault she kept tripping. Every time she stood up, we cheered and clapped. When she took few steps, we went wild!

You could tell she loved the applause; the kid already knows how to play to a crowd.

I think that since I've been working on *Shmirat Einayim* I've become more sensitive to success and failure. Believe me, I know how vulnerable I am. Despite all the progress I've made, I still seem to fall into the trap, over and over. Sometimes, I beat up on myself over it—control seems to be a goal that's forever receding ahead of me.

So I decided to take a tip from little Linda. She never loses confidence in herself when she falls. She doesn't get depressed or anxious either. Looking at her, I can picture her in my mind's eye just a year from now. Someday she'll walk, she'll run, she'll skip. She'll be in total control.

If she doesn't lose heart, neither should I. I can't let my failures get me down. It's the steady effort that counts. Sooner or later, I know it will pay off.

DAY

17

Design a
Strategic Plan

Dedicated by anonymous sponsors
for the success of their children.

*"One can assess the results of his business affairs, and then
try to rectify things before trouble occurs… We have the
ability to learn from our mistakes. To the degree that we
refuse to embrace foolishness, so will our wisdom increase."*

(Ohr Yisrael, Letter Four)

THE CONSEQUENCES OF business errors are clear because they cause financial loss, which is a powerful motivator. An entrepreneur makes every effort not to repeat his mistakes. "To embrace foolishness," means to make the same mistakes over and over. By refusing to do that, we become wiser.

---

*But life isn't like a business plan! What motivation can I use
to keep from repeating mistakes in Shmirat Einayim?*

Actually, the same rules for success apply in the *Shmirat Einayim* challenge. **The more you know about the detrimental effects of improper images, the more motivated you will be to avoid hurting yourself.** As a result, you will prepare yourself by having a plan.

Keep in mind that seeing immodest sights jeopardizes your spirituality and your ability to do *mitzvot*. Moreover, though it's unpleasant to think about, you have to face the fact that this pattern of *aveirot* will impact negatively on your eternal life in the World to Come.

Of course, these dire consequences are heavy and intimidating. But a realistic businessman squarely faces the possibility of bankruptcy should he fail to make the right decisions. In the same way, you don't want to spiritually bankrupt yourself. To be successful, you have to internalize the fact that viewing immodesty is costing you dearly in the spiritual world — the world that really counts ultimately.

What can you do? Create a plan! You can assess the downward spiral and take steps to end it with a strategy you design for yourself. Every person is different, but in general, these are the steps you should take each day before leaving home.

(1) Take a few moments to think about the prevalent practice of modern society to display improper images. Regard them as dangers that must be avoided.

(2) Think about what it will cost you spiritually should you be careless and not take precautions against these risks.

Review the four primary laws of Day 7. It will arm you against complacency and provide the guidelines you need.

As you develop sensitivity to your challenges, you will begin to identify your particular risks, and you will be able to personalize the specifics of your plan. You may need to make frequent adjustments to it. As in business, the environment is always changing, and your plan should change to accommodate new problems that arise.

TODAY: *Remember that society bombards us with indecent images, so prepare yourself before you leave home.*

STEVE'S JOURNAL...

On the way to my office yesterday, I inadvertently saw an indecent picture. The image lodged in my mind and I struggled with the effects all day. After lunch, I even had trouble concentrating on *Birkat Hamazon*.

I realized that for all my good intentions, I hadn't planned well enough to offset that particular risk. So I took a few minutes after I made my nightly 'spiritual accounting' to think about how I could have avoided it. I like to keep improving the strategies. It's like a chess game—the more I think about my next move, the better it will be.

Trying to come up with an effective strategy for avoiding pictures, I reviewed several pages of my spiritual log. I discovered that pictures are relatively rare challenges for me, but that I have a far more frequent pattern of failure right in my office building. That crowded elevator is still a problem.

So I came up with a plan. In the elevator tomorrow, I'll try to position myself behind a man and keep my eyes downward until I get to my floor, or maybe take the stairs.

When I think of this strategizing in the same light as

a business plan, I'm more alert to the daily changes. A few weeks ago, my company hired a new receptionist who doesn't dress professionally. I need to come up with a plan for coping with that new circumstance.

DAY

18

Implement Modest Dress at the Workplace

"Then Boaz said to his servant who was in charge of the reapers, 'Who is this woman?'"
(Ruth 2:5)

"Boaz noticed that Ruth conducted herself with unusual modesty. She sat while gathering the sheaves on the ground so she would not have to bend and expose her legs."
(Rashi)

IT APPEARS THAT even in ancient times, men and women working in close proximity resulted in *tzniut* issues. The Book of Ruth is set in Israel during the time of the Judges, when one would expect that such problems would not exist. Yet Ruth's modest behavior apparently was so unusual that Boaz recognized her spiritual nobility.

Today, society condones far greater latitude in clothing, creating issues that never would have arisen even a few decades ago. Can anything be done about it on an organizational level?

In my company, men and women work together all the time. Even though I own the company, I feel reluctant to impose my religious dress standards on my employees. Is there something I can do to encourage proper attire?

In many ways, the owner of a company is like a father figure to his employees. He provides them with an occupation so they can earn an honest livelihood. He understands that the better he treats his employees, the better they will fulfill their tasks. In the larger firms, the company provides health care packages, pension plans, and other benefits.

If you are an employer or a person of rank in your company, you serve as a role model, setting the standards for business ethics and personal integrity.

To create a healthy environment in your workplace you naturally encourage teamwork and good interpersonal relations. In this light, you surely want your office to be free of inappropriate conduct.

One of the most important factors contributing to a company's success is a respectful dress code. Immodest dress (of either gender) gives off a carefree, enticing message, which interferes with a business atmosphere and professionalism. It encourages flirtation which also could result in office scandals.

You might be thinking that as much as you want to establish a dress code, you feel that it is an inappropriate imposition on your employees. Just because you have your religious standards, is it fair to burden them with your restrictions?

Be aware that dress codes have been proven to be effective and necessary from a secular point of view. In an article titled, *Dress for Work Success: A Business Casual Dress Code* (Human Resources Newsletter) human resources expert Susan M. Heathfield writes, "Clothing that reveals too much… is not appropriate for a place of business, even in a business casual setting."

Today, dress codes are acceptable — and recommended — throughout the business world. Your employees have heard about dress codes from their friends and colleagues. They will not be offended or surprised if you tactfully ask them to dress appropriately. Dressing in a non-provocative manner is an important component in conducting oneself with dignity and morality. You owe this advantage to your employees, as well as to your customers who may be offended by lax standards.

What if you do not run your own business? As an employee, what can you do? One thing you might try is to look up some of the articles written on this topic and show them to your employer. Respectfully ask that he or she consider implementing rules of attire to boost company morale and productivity.

TODAY: *Whether you are an employer or an employee, consider the advantages of modest dress at the workplace and work to have them implemented.*

STEVE'S JOURNAL...

Remember the problem I had a while ago with my company's new receptionist? I thought of a way to deal with it. A dress code! If the dress regulations apply across the board to everyone, no one can be insulted when told to dress more professionally. The question in my mind was how to get this to happen. As a relatively new employee myself, I was the low man on the totem pole.

So I did a little research. It turns out that there are dozens of authoritative articles written on the subject. I made copies and took them in to my boss's office. I told him that a lot of us find inappropriate clothing distracting and that we would work better if everyone would dress more conservatively. (That is certainly true!)

At first, he gave me sort of a funny look, but he said he'd read them and consider my request. He was impressed by the articles and discussed the matter with the CEO. A few days letter, everyone in the company got this memo:

Research studies have shown that respectful dress improves efficiency between co-workers and creates a climate more conducive to productivity. Appropriate attire projects a professional image. In addition, it enhances the social ambiance of the office, creating a more pleasant and respectful atmosphere for all concerned.

We have decided to institute a dress code in our company. The code establishes a standard that is comfortable for everyone and it applies to both men and women.

We ask our employees not to wear jeans, sweat pants, shorts, or tee shirts.

Clothes should be clean and pressed.

Men should wear a button down shirt with dark colored slacks.

Women should avoid sheer fabrics and sleeveless blouses.

The neckline and the length of the skirt or dress should be conservative.

As always, suits are required for key meetings.

Whenever we interview a new employee, we will show this memo to him or her. Compliance is mandatory for all employees.

We have established a dress-code budget as an incentive for our employees to comply with our new dress code. Please see your supervisor to determine your needs.

That memo came out a few weeks ago. The receptionist came in the next day dressed in a decent outfit and—maybe it was my imagination—but she seemed to behave with more dignity too. Many clients have since complimented our company on our professional appearance and courteous interaction with our customers.

My boss got a bonus for suggesting the dress code to our CEO, and all I got was a nod and a smile. But I don't care—my objective was met!

DAY

19

Vanquish Improper Thoughts

Dedicated by David J. Jemal
in honor of his wife Wendy.

"Who is strong? One who subdues his passions."
(*Avot* 4:1)

*"A master of his passions is greater than
the conqueror of a city."*
(*Mishlei* 16:32)

*Rabbi Yisrael Salanter commented on these texts
with some of the most encouraging words of all time:
"Man has the ability to gain mastery over his nature. ...
Through Mussar study and force of habit,*
a person can transform himself."
(*Ohr Yisrael, Igeret HaMussar*)

IMAGINE BEING ABLE to transform yourself! Does that sound impossible? Rabbi Salanter tells us that it's possible even in areas that seem beyond our control, such as our thoughts.

I've been trying to control my eyes, but controlling my thoughts is beyond me. Besides, if a thought flashes through my mind, it doesn't mean anything. I can still control my behavior.

Most people are aware that it is inappropriate to have thoughts of desire for any woman, except for one's wife. Why? The basic reason is that improper thoughts defile our spirit and, in turn, cause misdeeds. So cutting off an improper thought is critically important. You may not think it will lead you to an *aveirah*, but the fact is that a thought is the first step to action. The Mishnah succinctly states, "An *aveirah* leads to another *aveirah*, and a *mitzvah* leads to another *mitzvah*." (*Avot* 4:2) From your own experience, you know this is true.

If your mind is full of improper desires, you will have a tendency to repeat that pattern. But if you succeed in conquering your *yetzer hara* — and **just one time** shut your eyes from seeing immodest images — it will be progressively easier for you to control your eyes *and* your thoughts. (*Sefer HaChinuch* 387 *Shelach*)

Chazal tell us that a desirous thought for a woman is "worse" than committing the illicit act (*Yoma* 29a). This means that thoughts of desire for a woman are a greater pleasure for a man than the illicit act, itself. What's more, since a thought is private, it is hard to motivate oneself to do *teshuvah* (i.e., repent) for it. In contrast, an actual improper action is tangible and (possibly) known, so it serves as a powerful impetus towards *teshuvah*. So in terms of spiritual regression, the thought is worse.

Let's look at the process more deeply. When a man looks with desire at a woman (who is not permitted to him), it causes spiritual impurity. But if a man cuts off the thought, the process reverses the negative streak and becomes the genesis of four good things:

(1) He protects his mind from *tumah*.

(2) He stops the inclination to commit an *aveirah*.

(3) He initiates good thoughts.

(4) He performs more and more good deeds because — as pointed out above — "One *mitzvah* leads to another *mitzvah*."

Cutting off the improper thought at its inception is known for this reason as "the root of all goodness." Even if a person is caught in a chain of improper thoughts, he can break the chain by cutting off his thoughts just once. Spiritual levels ascend progressively. The merit of controlling your eyes even one time will empower you to control your thoughts in the future and reach successive levels of *kedushah*.

TODAY: *Remember that by cutting off improper thoughts just once, you begin a new habit of control.*

STEVE'S JOURNAL...

Even though I'm learning to control my eyes (well, at least I'm trying), my mind still conjures thoughts that I'm not proud of. I'm being totally honest here. It seems to me that this is one war I will never win.

I got up the nerve to ask Rabbi Levy about it. After our class one morning, I told him that these thoughts creep in especially while I'm on my way to work. I'm doing my best, employing all the tactics I've learned not to look at improper sights, but I still see them in my mind's eye.

"Steve, you've got to fight fire with fire," he answered. When he saw my puzzled look, he explained. "A man has to fight the fire in his heart with the fire of Torah."

Then he opened up the *Mishnah Berurah* to chapter 98:2, where the Chofetz Chaim writes about how to control your thoughts. Rabbi Levy advised, "Here's how to deal with your problem. When you are walking through an immodest area, say to yourself verse 12 of Psalm 51, '*Elokim*, create a pure heart within me and renew my spirit.' Whether you say it in Hebrew or in English, just repeating the holy words of King David will uplift your soul. In addition, you'll be cutting off these improper thoughts by substituting words of Torah in your mind."

It seems to me that this technique is more than just diverting my thoughts. Those words are actually a short prayer. If I ask God to help me to keep my thoughts pure, it's a direct request. How could He turn that down?

DAY

20

Respect the Privacy of Other People

$$\boxed{20}$$

HERE'S A SIMPLE question. How would you feel if another man entertained immodest thoughts about your wife? Even if he were your best friend or relative, wouldn't you be offended? Then again, your wife is an attractive woman. Isn't your friend just having a normal human reaction?

The answer is obvious. Marital relationships are exclusively private. The Sages' word for marriage is *Kiddushin*, which means, "consecrated." Once married by Torah law, husband and wife are dedicated specifically to each other and set apart from everyone else. Their relationship is exclusive on every level. A Jewish wife is forbidden to every other man, except her own husband.

It stands to reason that if a man looks with desire at a married woman, even if she is modestly dressed, he is breaching the privacy of her relationship with her husband. The same respect must be shown to a modestly dressed woman who is single. Her beauty is reserved for the man she will eventually marry. Looking at her with desire will undoubtedly lead to impure thoughts.

This is why the law is so clear: "It is forbidden to derive pleasure from looking at the beauty of a woman, even if she is modestly dressed." (*Shulchan Aruch, Even HaEzer*, Chapter 21, Law 1)

In my professional life, I sometimes deal with women. Most of them dress conservatively, so I never thought there was a problem associated with looking at them. How can I function in the business world if I can't even look at a beautiful woman?

If you need to speak to a woman who is modestly dressed, first determine if you are able to speak to her while maintaining proper thoughts. If you decide that you can, remember to utilize everything you have learned up to now. And it's best to keep your time with her short, if possible.

The Talmud tells us that Rabbi Yirmiyah ben Abba once served as a witness for a loan. When the creditor came to collect the money, the rabbi did not recognize the woman who had borrowed it. The other witnesses told Rabbi Yirmiyah that it was the same woman, but she had aged. Was it that hard to recognize her? Abaye explained that it is not the nature of a Torah scholar to take particular note of a woman's face, which is why Rabbi Yirmiyah did not have a strong recollection of the incident. (*Bava Batra* 168a)

Although we are far from the holy status of Rabbi Yirmiyah ben Abba, we can learn from him. Even in situations that seem benign, we should not be overly attentive to the appearance of the women around us. As we learned on Day 10 in regard to balance in relating to women, this should be done with utmost care not to offend the women. You do not have to be obvious about it, nor look away suddenly or defensively.

With the wisdom of Torah and Mussar, you will find the inner reserves of strength and dignity to speak to modestly dressed women while retaining pure thoughts.

TODAY: *Respect the privacy of others by controlling your desires.*

STEVE'S JOURNAL...

I made an appointment with Mrs. Cohen to finalize the invitations for the shul dinner. The last time I was in her office she was dressed perfectly modestly. Nevertheless, I knew I had to take precautions to control my eyes.

But as I thought about going back again tomorrow, I decided that I should be able to do even better this time. After all, lately I've been sensitized to the laws of *Shmirat Einayim* and I'm working hard to keep my thoughts under control as well.

I took an honest look at how I would approach our meeting. She always dresses appropriately and there is something in her manner that is poised and dignified. That alone makes it easier for my thoughts concerning her to remain pure. So before going, I will review the laws and consciously have them in mind. I'm pretty sure that I can work with her "person to person," not male to female, keeping my mind focused on the task at hand.

This gives me a great feeling of control. Knowing that I can actually confront my nature and deal with it effectively has given me the confidence to deal with a situation like this. Good planning keeps me relaxed and upbeat. I feel a sense of integrity I never felt before.

It's like Dave said at the outset—little by little, all of this Mussar and Torah study is beginning to seep into my life. It still takes a lot of effort, but I'm beginning to see real progress.

DAY

21

Be Aware of the Enticing
Nature of the World

Dedicated by Joey Chehebar
in honor of my wife Deborah.

ON DAY 11, we discussed the importance of developing a deep awareness of Hashem. Another concept related to this is what Rabbi Salanter calls "Wisdom of the World."

"It is important to deepen our understanding of the ways of the world, which are deceptive. The various temptations of the world entrap people in their web, each person according to his own tendencies." [This understanding of the world is called Wisdom of the World.] (*Ohr Yisrael,* Letter Four)

I enjoy life and see the world as a beautiful place.
What is meant by the "deceptive nature" of the world?

It's true that G-d created a beautiful world. But it would be naïve for us to overlook the fact that seeing the world's enticements are the primary cause of sin and self-destruction. In fact, the very first episode in the Torah describes how Eve fell into deception and awesome devastation. The serpent urged her to eat the forbidden fruit so that she would gain true wisdom. While the serpent's enticement did awaken a desire to eat the fruit, it was not strong enough to convince her to violate G-d's commandment.

What convinced her to actually eat the fruit? She looked at the tree and it "was a delight to the eyes." (*Bereishit* 3:6) The *sight* of the fruit evoked a desire that overwhelmed her. She ate the fruit and then convinced Adam to eat it as well. As a result, death came into the world and they were both expelled from the Garden of Eden.

Throughout the Torah, we find examples of the power of vision to cause calamity. You may not have noticed this wording before. Here are a few examples:

◆ When Cain **saw** that only Abel's sacrifice was accepted by G-d, he was overcome with jealousy. He murdered his brother and suffered unspeakable consequences.

◆ When Ham **saw** his father, Noah, was unclothed, he disgraced him.

◆ When Lot **saw** the fertile plains of Sodom, he left Avraham and went to live there among evil people. He lost his spirituality and was nearly destroyed in the obliteration of Sodom.

◆ When Avimelech **saw** how beautiful Sarah was, he took her to his palace. He and his household were then stricken with a terrible illness.

◆ When Yosef's brothers **saw** that Yaakov gave him a special coat, they were blinded by envy. They sold their brother into slavery, greatly hurting Yaakov and tearing apart the family.

Samson was the strongest man, David the most pious, and Solomon the wisest. Nevertheless, each one of these great and holy men stumbled when caught in the gravitational field of a woman. (*Sefer Chasidim*)

If this danger existed in biblical times, how much more so is it prevalent in our times? Today, society exploits human weakness in order to manipulate others for its own benefit. Television, movies, advertisements, magazines, the entertainment industry and the internet use images of women to entice men. They have one goal: to increase sales. Showing a pretty woman is high on their list of sure ways to get a man's attention.

When we contemplate the powerful seductions that pulsate in the world around us, we start to attain the Wisdom of the World needed to help us control our eyes. This wisdom gives us the insight to live a wholesome life. This wisdom is gained by focusing on the following four strategies:

(1) **Recognize the enticing nature of the world.** For instance, as you walk through town, every fast-food place tries to tempt you: Sizzling steaks, mouth-watering ice cream, the tantalizing aroma of fresh coffee, chewy bagels, ice-cold coke, fresh pastry, and piping hot pizza. Yes, it's instant gratification, but at what a cost!

(2) **Understand that there are appetites in human nature that are triggered by sensory attractions.** What's more, it's very difficult to resist desire because desire is rooted in the subconscious. Before you smelled the pizza, you weren't even thinking about eating. But once the aroma hits your olfactory sense, your craving for pizza is aroused and you eat.

(3) **Know that surrendering to your cravings can be detrimental to your well-being.**

(4) **Prepare a plan in advance to protect yourself from being entrapped by your physical desires.**

TODAY: *Be aware of the enticing forces surrounding you. Guard your eyes from the images that try to manipulate your senses.*

STEVE'S JOURNAL...

Today we had a meeting with the marketing department to talk about how we will sell our new line of software. I had prepared what I thought was a pretty good mock-up of an ad, with a picture of the computer screen, pointing out all of the advantages of the new product. I even wrote a blurb about how it could give your business an edge over the competition. I showed it at the meeting. The marketing guys had a peculiar reaction to it.

"There's gotta be a girl in the picture," one of them replied, as though he were explaining it to a two-year-old. "Didn't you ever take Marketing 101 in college? It's basic."

"Yeah," another one said, "we want businessmen to really take a look. We need something they can't resist."

I was floored. I found myself stammering "But, but this is accounting software. There's no reason..."

"A secretary!" one of them shouted. "That's it! We show her using the software on her computer. She's smiling because it's so easy. We can put her boss standing near her, looking on approvingly ..."

I gave up. There was no arguing with them. But the whole incident made me stop and notice the advertising around me. Somehow, till I saw them actually scheming, the fact that marketing guys in every industry are manipulating me never sank in before. I felt like they had used the power of my own eyes against me, and I felt humiliated.

I can't change how these characters try to sell me their products, but from now on, I'll be smarter and not fall for their cheap tricks. They can't make me look.

DAY

22

Realize That "Private" Flaws Will Be Revealed

$$\boxed{22}$$

MIKE AND GAIL were married and lived in a vibrant observant community. They both came from traditional Orthodox families. Their goals were to build a Jewish home which reflected classic Torah ideals.

But just a few short years after they were married, Gail realized that Mike was viewing improper websites. Instinctively, she felt revolted and upset by this, and their relationship became strained. The couple decided to go for counseling, but Mike was not receptive to the advice offered by the counselor. Making matters even worse, Mike eventually stopped going to *shul* in the mornings. He showed little interest in maintaining the sanctity of their home or in strengthening their children's Torah education. Their family structure became completely unraveled.

It was painfully clear to Gail that she and her husband were no longer compatible. She did not want his influence in the house for her own sake as well as for the sake of their children. Not long after, Mike and Gail ended their marriage.

This true account (names changed) demonstrates how far "the eye" can lead a person from Torah values. The Talmud teaches that a person is led on the path that he truly wishes to go. If a person desires good, he will be inspired to do good. If he desires base things, he will be motivated towards unfavorable behavior. In Mike's case, his desire to look at improper images intensified until it became an obsession that eventually overwhelmed him.

Initially, he rationalized that his interest in the websites was "normal." He had no idea how viewing these sites weakened his soul, how little by little his inborn *kedushah* gave way, and *tumah* filled the vacuum. For quite a while, he was able to fake being a committed, observant Jew. Eventually, though, his *emunah* was affected and he became lax in observance. Subconsciously, he was still trying to rationalize his behavior, and he became inwardly cynical about Judaism. At this point, it became to clear to Gail what was happening, but she felt helpless. Still in denial, Mike rebuffed her efforts to discuss his problem. It wasn't until she insisted on a divorce, that he realized that his life was in shambles.

Had Mike known from the start that his desire would destroy his marriage, he would have reined it in immediately. To put it simply, Mike couldn't trust himself alone with a computer, so he should have seen to it that the opportunity wouldn't arise. He should have regarded privacy at his computer as tantamount to *yichud* [being alone] with a woman.

Wasn't Mike's problem unusual?
Do I need to worry about extremes?

You may believe that you are not a person likely to fall into such a trap, but consider Rabbi Yisrael Salanter's insightful words on the subject:

> Each person has certain blind spots in his personality. For instance, a spendthrift will waste money on items which are completely unnecessary. A compulsive eater will eat everything that looks good despite the effect on his health. (*Ohr Yisrael*, Letter Four)

Imagine a judge who is a great legal scholar but has little understanding of the deceptive tactics that people use to manipulate others. If a defendant lies in court, this judge might not be able to see through it. But if the judge has "street-smarts" as well as knowledge of the law, he will recognize the deceptions of the defendant and render a just ruling.

Just as the judge who is unfamiliar with deception is unable to recognize it, so too, we don't see how vulnerable we are to visual stimulation unless we've been sensitized to realize its effect. Fact: When a man looks at a woman, his desire becomes ignited. *Chazal* expressed this truth thousands of years ago, and it is still just as true today: "The eye sees and then the heart desires."

If you think you are above being overwhelmed by desire, think again. Bad habits form slowly. Only alertness — and the knowledge that inevitably "private" flaws will be revealed — can give you the ability to intercept them.

TODAY: *Put the story of Mike and Gail into your mental arsenal to serve as an effective deterrent to viewing improper sights.*

STEVE'S JOURNAL...

Yesterday I found out about Mike and Gail's divorce. Mike was a good friend of mine, but I never knew what was happening, until it was over. At first, they made it sound like it was due to some sort of incompatibility, but the real story went around our circle pretty fast. Secrets melt in the glare of a divorce.

At first, I didn't believe it. Mike and I were raised in the same kind of home and we went to the same yeshivah. In fact, I always admired him. He was a good student and spent a couple of years learning Torah before going into business. It turns out that his bad habit started slowly, and only Gail knew about it.

You'd think he would have been smart enough to see this coming. What I don't understand is why he continued, even after his family life started to fall apart.

I thought a lot about how their whole family is suffering. What can I take out of this? I guess that most of us don't see ourselves too clearly. Even though it seems like a bizarre possibility—if it can happen to him, it could happen to me.

I can't forget about poor Mike! He's lost so much. I hope he can still clean up his act and get on with his life.

DAY

23

Control Your Home Environment

I F YOU ARE an employee, you probably have little control over your work environment. Short of requesting a respectable dress code, there may be little you can do that will influence the entire company.

Several years ago, a popular anti-*lashon hara* campaign included desktop placards that warned, "Don't even think of telling me *lashon hara.*" It stopped gossip-mongers in their tracks, at least in the immediate vicinity of the people who put up the sign. Without being obnoxious or "holier-than-thou" about it, you can convey the same distaste for immodesty. Simply walk away silently when inappropriate jokes or pictures emerge. Fairly soon, your co-workers will get the message and will not bother including you in that kind of "fun." You may even find that they respect you more for the sincerity of your Jewish integrity.

My wife and I make a solid effort to make the environment in our home Jewish, but I never thought of this in light of Shmirat Einayim.

Your home can be a spiritual oasis, free of improper sights and full of Torah study and *mitzvot*. The *kedushah* and purity of such a home nurtures the souls that live in it. It radiates with the special love of Jewish parents and it is the very foundation of *Klal Yisrael*. This home will abound with blessings of peace, happiness, and closeness to Hashem.

When you were first married, this was what you wanted. But over the years, laxness creeps in and standards change. You may have lost sight of the goal. No matter what the ages of your children — even if you do not have children — you can start now to make your home the spiritual oasis your family deserves.

What can you do? First, set a good example. Do you dress with the same modesty inside as you do outdoors? Do you behave in a modest fashion? Is your language clean?

What sort of influences do you allow within the four walls of your home? Without our realizing it, immodest images appear daily in store circulars and unsolicited mail. Be on the alert for these, and eliminate them from your environment.

Secular educators as well as religious leadership have recognized that the media is a destructive influence on virtually every individual. If you stop to notice these negative influences in your home life and decide that they need to be modified, view it as an educational opportunity.

The great Rabbis of our generation have ruled that internet should not be allowed in the home unless it is required for business — and *only* used for that purpose. If you have a question whether or not your situation allows internet in the home, consult with a *halachic* authority for guidance.

Don't simply forbid this or that. This is an opportunity to discuss with your children why these influences are objectionable. What messages do they convey? How do they conflict with our values? Don't lecture — discuss.

The Midrash teaches that Hashem instructed Moshe exactly how to count the Jewish nation. He told him to go to each tent and count how many souls were in each family. But Moshe did not invade their privacy. He stood at the entrance of each tent and the *Shechinah* "entered" the household. A heavenly voice then told him the number of children inside.

What can we learn from this Midrash? If we are worthy, Hashem comes into our homes, just as one visits his friend! He loves us so much that He wants to be with us. But our homes must be ready for His Presence. We can do that by maintaining a home free of immodest images and by raising our children to be aware that they are endowed with a noble spiritual status. Every Jewish family should be sensitive to the fact that much of the language and entertainment popular today are beneath us. It is the parents who demonstrate and guard this reality.

TODAY: *Take steps to control the spiritual atmosphere of your home. Make your home a fitting place to receive the Shechinah.*

STEVE'S JOURNAL...

Sara and I decided to discuss what we could do to improve our home environment. Now that Eddie is 14, Julie is 11, and Raymond is 8, they are more subject to the cultural influences around us than ever before. We agreed that the environment is a lot worse today than it was when we were kids.

We realized that there's really no way we can always monitor what they see and hear when they're out of the house, but our home should be a place where modesty is the norm and the richness of our Jewish life is dominant.

We called a family meeting to talk about it. The kids were less than thrilled when they found out the topic I wanted to discuss. Eddie drummed his fingers on the table, Julie rolled her eyes and Raymond just sat there open-mouthed. I started by asking them what's Jewish about our home — if a stranger walked in, how could he tell it's a place where observant Jews live? They looked around and started pointing out *mezuzot*, our Chanukah menorah, Sara's Shabbat candlesticks, the Jewish books and *siddurim*.

"Now, what's not Jewish about our home?" They were stuck. "Um, some of our CD's?" ventured Eddie. "Maybe the movie star posters in my room?" suggested Julie.

The conversation wasn't easy, but we discussed why these influences don't belong in our lives, and I confessed that I had been careless to let them in. When I suggested that we all take a break from watching TV for a while, Raymond whined,

"We'll die!"

"You don't mean completely, do you, Dad?" questioned Eddie.

"Yes, completely."

"Even your evening news, Dad?" he said craftily. I nodded yes, even the news. The kids looked from one to the other.

"That's so mean," muttered Julie under her breath. "I can't believe we're doing this."

I didn't blink. Sara smiled. "It won't be easy for any of us, but I think that as a family we can kick the TV habit together. Let's try!"

We knew they would have a lot of extra time on their hands, so the next day, we went shopping together. We helped Eddie buy the telescope he'd been saving up for; we got paint supplies for Julie so she could take art lessons; and we let Raymond pick a hobby. Now he has everything he needs to start a rock and mineral collection.

DAY

24

Provide a Spiritual Inheritance for Your Children

Thank You Hashem, for giving us Torah tools to improve our lives! Please bless my wonderful community and the entire Jewish People.

I S THERE ANYTHING more beautiful than sitting with your family at the Shabbat table and discussing *Parshat HaShavuah?* Each one of us wants to see the continuity of a Torah lifestyle in our children. While there are many factors that contribute to their spiritual wellbeing, much of the results depend on our own level of commitment.

> *What is the relationship between Shmirat Einayim and the success of my children in living a lifestyle of Torah values?*

Numerous Torah sources attest to the remarkable mechanism that Hashem implemented in this world — the fact that children benefit spiritually from the actions of their parents. Think of it as spiritual DNA. The *Midrash Bereishit Rabbah* (128:18) hints at the transmission of *kedushah* from one generation to the next:

When Yosef went forth to rule over Egypt, the daughters of kings used to gaze at him through the lattice and throw jewelry so that he would lift up his eyes and look at them. Yet he did not look at them! Hashem said to him, ["Because you did not look at the ornaments thrown to get your attention] I will give *your daughters* an ornament in the Torah." What ornament? [They will have] a portion in the Torah.

Just as Yosef's modest behavior blossomed with merit for his future offspring, so too, our actions affect not only our own spiritual nature, but that of our descendents as well.

How does this mechanism work? Let's take a close look at another Torah source. In *Mishlei* (20:7) it is recorded, "The *tzaddik* walks in his perfection — happy are the children after him." The meaning of the phrase, "The *tzaddik* walks in his perfection" means that the *tzaddik* worked hard to fulfill a *mitzvah* or to develop a worthy character trait. As a result, Hashem will bless his children **so that they can reach that level with much less effort.** Their father made the spiritual breakthrough for them, so "happy are the children after him."

The more we dedicate ourselves to Torah observance, the more we enhance the *kedushah* of our children. Conversely, if we allow our Torah observance to weaken, we diminish our children's spiritual resilience.

Physical traits are transmitted to the child from his inception by DNA coding. Rabbi Eliyahu Dessler writes in his *Michtav M'Eliyahu*, that spiritual traits are transmitted both in the womb and after the child is born. If a parent achieves a particular character virtue — even after the child is born — this good trait will be transmitted to the child. It will be easier for the child to master his nature regarding that same challenge. One of the most powerful ways to guarantee that your children follow a lifestyle of *mitzvot* is to strengthen your own commitment. When you develop control over your eyes, you are helping to build the spiritual foundation of your children.

This is easier said than done, to be sure. As discussed in earlier chapters, the internet poses a particular challenge, one that our parents didn't have. The fact that it is so useful is partly what makes it so dangerous. Our children find themselves in the middle of a great spiritual tug-of-war, where countless mesmerizing and pervasive negative attractions flash in front of them. With one click, they could begin a downward spiral that eventually will lead them far away from Torah values. They need your protection!

TODAY: *Help your children and future generations by controlling your eyes. Grant them "a spiritual inheritance" empowering them with the capability to preserve the well-being of their souls.*

STEVE'S JOURNAL...

Today I had a lunch date with a client and he took me to the new kosher restaurant a few blocks from my office. The food was great, but the atmosphere was charged with distractions. Some of the waitresses were not dressed modestly.

Dave and I had recently learned that overcoming my *Shmirat Einayim* challenge benefits not only me, but my children as well. The idea blows me away!

It's a very deep concept, and I don't claim to understand it. But what I took away from our discussion was that I'm not in this just for myself. Every time I control my eyes, I'm empowering my kids (maybe even my grandkids!) to do better in this area. It's a concrete way that I can give them a spiritual advantage.

Now that's a powerful motivator. So when I encountered the waitress, I buried my eyes in the menu. "Do this for Julie," I told myself.

"Can I take your order?" she asked. I asked my client to order first, then, without looking up, I gave my order. As she was walking away, I looked down to drink a glass of water. Then I asked my client if he would mind if I changed my seat, and I placed myself in the chair facing the wall instead of the interior of the restaurant.

Somehow, the fact that my children will get some sort of spiritual boost out of my restraint made it a whole lot easier. But in the future, I'm taking my clients to my good ol' restaurant down the block where my regular waiter—Brad—will be happy to serve us.

DAY

25

Remember
Your Heritage

A FASCINATING INSIGHT FOUND in *Midrash Tanchuma* (*Vayeshev*) is that the righteous and the wicked both use their sense of sight, but for different purposes.

"*Tzaddikim* **elevate** themselves with their eyes, as it says (*Bereishit* 22:4), 'And Avraham lifted up his eyes and *saw* the place from afar.' Regarding Yitzchak, it says (*Bereishit* 24:63): 'And Yitzchak went out to the field in the evening and he *saw*...' About Yaakov, it says (*Bereishit* 33:1): 'And Yaakov lifted up his eyes and *saw*...'

"But wicked people **fall** due to their eyes, as it says (*Bereishit* 13:10): '...and Lot lifted his eyes and he *saw* the entire plane of Jordan.' This is Sodom. He left Avraham and went to Sodom in order to follow after their bad deeds. Regarding Balak, it says (*Bamidbar* 22:2): 'And Balak ben Zippor *saw*...' [and eventually sought to curse the Nation of Israel]."

We all have the G-d-given ability to choose. Every organ and limb can be used constructively, but it can also be used to degrade ourselves and destroy. The moral choice is ours.

What tools can I use to make sure I make the best choices?

Fortunately, we have several weapons at our disposal to help us choose to do the right thing. The combination of our awareness of Hashem (*Yirat Shamayim*, discussed on Day 11) and Wisdom of the World (the concept that we must be aware of traps in the world, discussed on Day 21) complement each other in the "battle of the eyes." These are powerful deterrents and they are even more effective when you **realize who you are** — the son of Avraham, Yitzchak, and Yaakov.

We can learn a lot from Yaakov's son, Yosef. It's worth the time reviewing the biblical story. During the time that Yosef was a slave in Egypt, he was appointed household caretaker of an Egyptian government official named Potiphar. Here he encountered a great test. Potiphar's wife was extremely attracted to Yosef and brazenly tried to seduce him at every opportunity. Yosef's automatic response was to turn away to avoid seeing her. His first line of defense was his intense awareness of Hashem, and it was effective for quite some time in neutralizing her efforts.

Only after repeated attempts over a long period of time was she able to find a chink in his spiritual armor. Nevertheless, Yosef immediately recovered and saved himself from sinning. What did he do?

(1) He saw the image of his father's face.

(2) He ran away from the palace.

Seeing the image of the face of Yaakov, reminded him that he was the descendent of great *tzaddikim*. It would be beneath his dignity and moral heritage for him to yield to this woman. These thoughts injected him with the strength to bolster his waning awareness of Hashem and helped him gain control.

Why did he run outside? That was the best way of removing Potiphar's wife from his sight. In both of these actions — picturing his father and running outside — he was using what we call Wisdom of the World. He was savvy enough to know that her seduction must be met by determined thought and action.

You, too, are descended from the very same *tzaddikim* as Yosef. In addition, you are heir to generations of ancestors who sacrificed much to maintain their Judaism. In addition to direct ancestors, you are also the beneficiary of generations of *tzaddikim* of our great nation. If your eyes are challenged and your *Yirat Shamayim* is not sufficient, think of the greatest *tzaddik* you ever met and imagine how he would behave in this situation. Imagine how your ancestors would feel if they could see you now. Know that Hashem is watching you too, as indeed He is.

Rabbi Yisrael Salanter noted that most of us know intellectually that Hashem sees our actions, but the full consciousness of this truth has not yet penetrated our hearts. Our main defense must be Wisdom of the World. In letter 4 of *Ohr Yisrael*, he writes:

"Wisdom of the World will lighten our burden and the awareness of Hashem will strengthen us."

Each one us has fluctuating degrees of *Yirat Shamayim*. As you continue your efforts to master your eyes, you will learn how to increase your awareness of Hashem and apply the Wisdom of the World. And, like Yosef, you will be able to withstand challenges using these tools and by knowing that you are descended from morally strong forefathers.

TODAY: *Think about your heritage and internalize its meaning. Along with your awareness of Hashem and Mussar study of the Wisdom of the World, it will help you in your battle for Shmirat Einayim.*

STEVE'S JOURNAL...

On the train this morning, I found myself surrounded by immodesty. It felt like the whole world had conspired to weaken my *Yirat Shamayim*, and I realized that I was losing the battle.

I wasn't strong enough to control my eyes. So I tried to think of everything I could to combat this impulse: I thought about Mike and Gail, and how their marriage fell apart when he lost control of his eyes. I thought about Eddie and Julie and Raymond, and how I must be strong for their sakes as well as mine.

Once I was thinking of my family, my mind conjured images of my grandfather, *zichrono l'vrachah*. I could see him perfectly in my mind's eye, sitting on the back porch in that regal blue bathrobe of his. What a magnificent person he had been! He treasured his life of Torah and *mitzvot* so much that he had fled from his anti-Semitic hometown as a boy to preserve it. He used to tell us a lot about those days. Though he never lectured us, there was something about him that demanded respect for the purity of his life and the genuineness of every *mitzvah* he did. He got that from his father, I suppose. He had the warmest smile.

I realized that I come from a long line of noble Jews. That thought suddenly gave me a sense of dignity and I somehow felt that the temptations around me were not worthy of my attention. So I pulled a book out of my briefcase, one I carry for this very purpose. I had chosen it one day when I realized that there are circumstantial traps like this one. It helped me distract myself from the people around me.

Grandpa would have been proud.

DAY

26

Employ the Power of Viewing Holy Things

"How wonderful it would be if we could channel the energy of our lesser personality traits to serve Hashem."

(*Ohr Yisrael*, Letter Four)

Can my desire to see improper images be re-channeled to strengthen me spiritually?

D ID YOU KNOW that just as the eye is stimulated by negative images it is also stimulated by positive images? Our Sages tell us that if we focus on holy objects, simply viewing them will instill holiness within us and inspire us to perform the *mitzvot* better.

For instance, can there be anything more inspiring than viewing a beautiful sunrise, a colorful flower or the graceful flight of a bird? All of these sights reflect the majesty of the Creator.

Moreover, our Sages tell us that when we gaze upon holy objects, the light of our eyes brightens and increases. Listed below are some of the holy things we can view that have positive effects on us.

(1) When you look at the face of a *tzaddik,* your soul is

illuminated with light and holiness. (*Degel Machaneh Ephraim*)

(2) Looking at the *sefer Torah* when it is raised before or after *kriat haTorah* — and reading a word or two from the scroll — imparts a great, holy light to us. (*Magen Avraham*, chapter 134)

(3) Viewing the *shin* on either side of the *Tefillin shel Rosh* imparts holiness.

(4) Looking at water is good for the eyes. (*Ibn Ezra*)

(5) Looking at the heavens imparts *Yirat Shamayim*. (The Vilna Gaon)

(6) When reciting the *Kriat Shema* in *Shacharit*, it is good to look at the *tzitzit* and touch them to the eyes when you say, *u'reitem o'toh*. (*Shulchan Aruch* 24:4)

(7) Whoever brings the *tzitzit* to his eyes when saying *Parshat Tzitzit* will never lose his sight. (*Be'er Hetev*)

(8) Looking at the *tzitzit* inspires one to perform *mitzvot* and stops him from randomly following his eyes. We should look at our *tzitzit* a few times a day. This is especially important and beneficial if an impure thought enters your heart. (*Shmirat HaLashon* — [Chafetz Chaim] 2:30)

(9) Before saying *Kiddush* on Shabbat night, look at the candles. While saying *Kiddush*, look into the wine cup. (*Shulchan Aruch* 271:10)

(10) Whenever leaving the house, look at the *mezuzah* and kiss it. (*Ma'aseh Rav HaChadash*)

(11) It is a *mitzvah* to watch other people who are performing a *mitzvah*, just as it was a *mitzvah* to watch

the *Kohen Gadol* perform his *Avodah* on Yom Kippur. (*Nefesh Kol Chai Phelagi*)

(12) If you look at a synagogue or a *Beit Midrash* you will be spiritually elevated — how much more so if you enter the building. You will be even more elevated if you stand in front of the Ark and look at the holy Torah. (*Rosh HaGivah*)

(13) Looking at the four-letter name of G-d — *YHVH* — and visualizing it is a great spiritual influence and enhances *Yirat Shamayim*.

(14) Study of the holy Torah imparts holiness, light, and joy to your soul.

TODAY: *Take the opportunity to look at holy sights and know that your soul is uplifted by them.*

STEVE'S JOURNAL...

A few nights ago, Dave pointed out something important to me. He noticed that as we continued to explore methodologies to safeguard *Shmirat Einayim*, I began to go overboard in my attitude — I began to think that it's impossible to look at anything!

"Steve, your eyes are not your enemy!" he said.

"Did I say they are?"

"In so many words, yes. You don't have to be afraid of using your sight. Think of your eyes as a window to inspiring, illuminating sights. Use them to your advantage."

"Like a tourist trying to take in all the beauty of a foreign country."

"Yeah, sort of."

So I began to think of how to do "spiritual sightseeing." The first thing I started doing was to let my eyes consciously rest on my *tefillin* before I put them on each day. I made it a point to look inside the Torah as it was being held up during services in the synagogue. When I pass the *Beit Midrash* on my way to the train in the morning, I peek inside and catch a glimpse of people learning Torah. On my way home after work, I watch the sun set.

These are small things and each only takes a few seconds. Yet I found that I'm uplifted by them. Maybe it's the increasing awareness of the spirituality around me, I don't know. All I know is that I feel more connected to G-d and the intrinsic holiness at my fingertips — and there is nothing quite like it.

DAY

27

Guide a Friend

"Another effective way of mastering ourselves is to instruct a friend and guide him towards goodness. ... If we study the ways of human nature in order to understand the paths of man and his falseness — this study of 'Wisdom of the World' has the power to correct all inappropriate behavior and improper thoughts."

(*Ohr Yisrael*, Letter Four)

It's hard for me to believe that guiding others will help me correct my own inappropriate behavior and improper thoughts.

L IKE A GENERAL encouraging his soldiers on the eve of battle, Rabbi Yisrael Salanter encourages us with words of inspiration, wisdom, and hope. He now reveals another stratagem to ensure your triumph over your *yetzer hara:* convey these ideas to a friend. Your approach must be custom tailored to each person, according to his particular personality, values, and culture. By understanding his inner makeup before you attempt to discuss this topic with him, you will be able to approach him sensitively and effectively.

Rabbi Salanter urges you to "guide him to goodness." This means you can inspire your friend and encourage him by explaining that you know of a worthwhile strategy for mastering his eyes. Every Jewish soul yearns for holiness. He may be more willing to undertake this project than you anticipate.

By articulating your convictions and knowledge to others, you will clarify and reinforce them in yourself. You will review the dangers of letting your eyes rove and will increase your efforts to control them. Rabbi Salanter goes so far as to say that by guiding others **you will be transformed, attaining levels of *mitzvot* and holy thoughts that you previously thought were not within your reach.**

Another spiritual mechanism goes into operation as well: the Torah concept of *middah k'neged middah*, measure for measure. When we help others achieve spiritual well-being, G-d helps us achieve it too. Rabbi Yisrael taught, "In order to heal himself, a person should bring merit to others by influencing them to attain *Yirat Shamayim* and the wisdom of Mussar. And the Talmud teaches, 'All who have mercy on other people, Heaven will have mercy on them.' There is no greater compassion [for other human beings] than influencing others to study Mussar."

TODAY: *Show this guidebook to a friend and offer to study it with him.*

STEVE'S JOURNAL...

I decided to buy a little gift for Dave because I really appreciate the time he spends learning Mussar with me.

I went to the Hebrew bookstore and bought him a gift certificate. When I gave it to him, though, his reaction was puzzled.

"Thanks, so much, Steve," he finally said, "but I don't understand why you did this."

"I just want to thank you for all the time we spend learning together."

"But I'm learning this for myself as much as for you," he protested. "It's doing just as much good for me as for you."

I had thought he was just being nice, helping me win my particular battle. It never occurred to me that there was something in it for him.

"Since we started learning about *Shmirat Einayim* together, I'm much less apt to slip up," he explained. "And somehow, by explaining it to you, I clarify these issues for myself too. You should try it. Who do you know who could benefit from learning about this?"

Now it was my turn to object. "Hey, I'm no master! Who am I to teach *Shmirat Einayim* to anybody? I'm not that good at it myself!"

"You don't have to be perfect. Share something good with someone else. You'll see; it will give you more strength."

I thought of my friend Sam, a guy I know at work. He's got the same challenges in the office that I do. I know him to be a sincere Jew; more than once he's mentioned that he wishes he had more time for Torah study. Maybe he'd like to take in a little Mussar on our lunch-break.

DAY

28

Don't Be Discouraged

I T'S EASY TO become discouraged if you work in an environment where you must constantly be on guard. Don't give in!

> *You can say, "just don't look," but I am surrounded by immodestly dressed people every day. Sometimes I think it's hopeless to try to avoid them.*

Consider the account in the Talmud (*Ta'anit* 21b) about Abba, a doctor who received daily "greetings" from Heaven. What was his special merit? He had separate rooms for his male and female patients. Moreover, he would take serious precautions to guard his eyes when he treated women. These acts were considered such an accomplishment that he was given this rare spiritual reward.

A person who is regularly confronted with improper sights and controls his eyes is considered by G-d to be a mighty warrior. Your Creator is fully aware of the challenges He sends your way, and overcoming this one is no small achievement. That is why our Sages tell us that you will be rewarded for averting your eyes with abundant blessing in this world, as well as in the World to Come. [*Taharat HaKodesh*]

According to *Taharat HaKodesh*, if a person controls his eyes when he is in public places, Heaven considers it as if he withstood a test as difficult as Joseph's with the wife of Potiphar. Because he triumphed on that occasion and was known for his continual emphasis on modest behavior, he is known as Yoseph HaTzaddik. When we emulate his behavior, we are rewarded with the same blessings he received.

Taharat HaKodesh also offers an illuminating thought on a verse in the Song of Songs (5:12): "His eyes are as the eyes of a dove, by springs of water":

> A dove has only one mate for his entire lifetime. If the men of Israel will not look at other women besides their wives, they will be likened to the Holy Supernal Dove, [i.e. G-d Himself]. In addition, they are "by springs of water," as it says (in Isaiah 58:11), "You will be like a watered garden and like a spring of water, whose waters do not fail." The allusion to water depicts wisdom and understanding.

TODAY: *Reinforce your resolve to guard your eyes in public places and know that you will receive a special blessing from G-d for your efforts.*

STEVE'S JOURNAL...

As I came into my office this morning, my eyes fell upon an attractive woman waiting in the reception area. She was in my visual field for only a few seconds—but it was long enough for me to feel like a failure. After all my study, all my talk about *Shmirat Einayim*! I had fallen into the trap like an unsuspecting schoolboy.

I trudged into my office, beating up on myself as a hypocrite. A few minutes later, the phone rang. It was Dave. Is the guy psychic or something? I told him that I'm ready to give up—this challenge is simply too much for me.

He listened patiently as he always does. When I finished ranting, he said quietly, "What makes you think you're different from everybody else? We all fail once in a while. It doesn't make you a hypocrite, only human."

That was cold comfort. It didn't help me to know that others are overwhelmed too. But Dave wasn't finished. "Let me give you a little secret weapon," he offered. "Whenever you're confronted by a challenge like this, remember Yoseph HaTzaddik. He almost gave in to temptation too, but he overcame it. If you put in that extra ounce of effort, you will be putting yourself on his level—and the rewards are just as great."

"No way."

"I have it on good authority. Don't be discouraged. You may have trying moments, but don't let them get to you. When you work hard at this, your effort is rewarded in ways you can't even imagine."

So I felt better, determined to keep trying. One thing I know: When G-d promises blessings, He always delivers. Every now and then, I need that shot in the arm.

DAY

29

Understand the Purpose of This Challenge

O NE OF THE most important things to know when an improper sight is imposed upon your view is that its grip on you *will* fade! The sight could trigger an intense reaction in your mind. You might even think, "I can't shake this." Don't allow the force of imagination to rule over you. It is an illusion, a mirage.

How can I gain control of the situation? And, come to think of it, why do I have this problem in the first place?

Remember that your attention to the mental image is the only fuel that keeps it alive. Simply let it pass and it will dissipate and vanish. Like flipping the page of a book, you can switch the focus of your mind. Force your mind to turn that page.

The classic Mussar work, *Mesilat Yesharim* (*Path of the Just*) by Rabbi Moshe Chaim Luzzato (*Ramchal*), tells us that G-d placed us in a physical realm with many things that distract us from coming close to Him. Why would He do that? There are a good many Mussar works that probe that very question, and you may want to look further for a deeper discussion of this topic. The short answer, however, is that G-d put man on this earth as a creature with free choice — *bechirah*. He wants us to exercise this G-dly trait in order to serve Him with conscious intent, not as robots or angels that must do as they are told. So He gives us choices to make — real choices in the form of challenges.

The very first chapter of *Mesilat Yesharim* expresses this concept: *The purpose of man in this world is to fulfill mitzvot, serve Hashem and withstand tests.*

Our mission is to use our power of choice to win the war of *kedushah* over desire. When you choose to align yourself with *kedushah* — no matter how many setbacks you've had — you will arrive triumphantly in the World to Come. You will have used your lifetime to come closer to Hashem, the true desire of the soul, and in the process became spiritually fulfilled. In the next world, the dimension after death, that fulfillment takes the form of intense spiritual pleasure, expanding eternally.

Rabbi Luzzato states our lifetime purpose in this way:

Man was only created in order to delight in Hashem and take pleasure from the Divine Presence, which is the true pleasure of all the pleasures that can be found.

His enlightening explanation of the purpose of pleasure in this world is written in lofty terms:

The purpose of pleasures in this world is only to assist a person in having calmness and peace of mind so that he can turn his heart to serve Hashem. It is fitting that everything he does should be dedicated to the Creator.

This may seem like a daunting, unrealistic goal. On an average day, how many of us think of our Creator at all (except when praying), much the less "dedicate everything" we do to Him? Is *Mesilat Yesharim* intended only for pious *tzaddikim*?

In actuality, Rabbi Luzzato is inferring that every Jew can aspire to high levels of thought and behavior: our capability for it is programmed into our spiritual DNA. No one can instantly reach this goal. It takes a lifetime. But you should be aware that in spiritual realms, all of your efforts are noted and rewards are tallied. If you think that you are at too low a level — that you don't qualify for Divine notice — consider the following facts that we learn from our Sages.

(1) When you avert your eyes from looking at an improperly dressed woman, you merit "receiving the *Shechinah*." (*Chazal Derech Eretz*) This means that the moment you guard your eyes from looking at an improper sight, you receive the *Shechinah,* even if you do not sense it.

(2) Each time you avoid an improper sight, you are considered a "holy person" and G-d rewards you for performing this *mitzvah.*

(3) Cutting off an improper thought, even just once, is "the root of all goodness" because it changes the trajectory of your thoughts and actions. (See Day 19.)

(4) According to *Taharat HaKodesh*, in the World to Come you will see the glorious *Shechinah* in the

merit of averting your eyes **even one time**. Imagine if you avert your eyes continually!

TODAY: *Draw closer to Hashem — now and forever — by controlling your eyes. Internalize the idea that your soul is benefitting from your restraint, whether or not you sense it.*

STEVE'S JOURNAL...

Today I went to buy flowers for Shabbat—a sweet, simple *mitzvah*, right? But I was thrown for a loop when the pretty clerk told me that the flowers I chose need special treatment. She started giving me detailed instructions. I was unprepared for this and struggled to listen without staring at her. I focused my eyes on the flowers.

A few weeks ago, I would have considered this experience discouraging because I had to struggle so hard to avert my attention from her. But I guess all of that Mussar study is finally kicking in. I gained control of the situation, remembering that the effort itself draws me closer to Hashem.

When it comes to *Shmirat Einayim*, I know that I've grown and improved. I don't want recognition for it from anyone. It's between G-d and I. Only we know how hard this is for me and how far I've come.

DAY

30

Perform the Mitzvot with Joy!

Dedicated by an anonymous sponsor.

30

THE ARIZAL ONCE revealed that the lofty spiritual levels he attained and the esoteric knowledge that he received were the result of his great happiness in serving Hashem.

How can we utilize the various ideas that we learned concerning Shmirat Einayim to serve Hashem with great joy?

All the *mitzvot* that we perform connect us to the infinite and pleasurable wellspring of Hashem's abundant blessings. Each effort we make to control our eyes is the fulfillment of an important *mitzvah*. Therefore, every time we control our eyes we link ourselves to the ultimate benefit as well as eternal reward. The greater our awareness of the eternal blessings flowing upon us with each *mitzvah* that we do, **the greater happiness, delight, and joy we will experience.**

We have completed the guidebook, *Windows of the Soul*. Now we have the wisdom, tools, and confidence to master our eyes.

For sure, now that we have many "tools in our toolbox," we have a great assortment of highly effective ways to control our eyes. Now you can "score many points" each time that you utilize one of the techniques that we have learned. We have the power now to convert each visual challenge into a great resource of spiritual growth, holiness, blessing, and reward.

The Ramchal wrote in *Mesilat Yesharim* (Introduction): "The benefit of this book is not gained by reading it one time, for it is possible that the reader won't find many ideas that he didn't already know. Rather the benefit from the book is gleaned from review and consistent study. In this way, the study of the book will remind him of concepts that are naturally forgotten by people. And he will remember his obligations which may have eluded him."

Mastery of the eyes requires reviewing the laws and consistent study of the pertinent topics. Therefore, keep the book with you and go through it periodically. Now that you know much of the ideas, you might prefer to read the book straight through in a few sittings. Or perhaps, turn to key parts that address the specific issues at hand.

In addition, you can study the book with a partner or ask your Rabbi to give a class on *Shmirat Einayim,* using the sources of his choice.

GROWING WISE

"THE CREATION OF man was for his ultimate existence in the World to Come. Therefore, Hashem endowed him with a precious soul. With his soul he is able to serve Hashem and to receive his eternal reward in its right time and place. Therefore, the existence of the soul in this world is beloved and pleasant to the soul." (*Mesilat Yesharim, Man's Duty in his World*):

Each word of Torah study, each second of contemplation and each effort we make to control our eyes will uplift and sanctify us. There is no greater joy than attaining holiness and purity!

May Hashem bless your efforts to master your eyes. May our collective effort to serve Hashem awaken great mercy in Heaven, so that we merit seeing the redemption of Klal Yisrael and the restoration of the *Shechinah* to the Kodesh HaKadashim.

"May Yisrael rejoice in its Maker; let the children of Zion rejoice in their King." (*Tehillim* 149:2)

Concise Guidelines to Internet Filters

Rabbi Eliezer Man Shach, zz"l said: "One of the most important responsibilities of parents is to provide their children with a warm, loving, and emotionally supportive home. With this foundation children are able to develop the fortitude to resist outside negative influences. Parents who do not do this are destroying the soul of their children. Giving warmth and love is the most important factor in Jewish education."

In a similar fashion, Rav Shlomo Wolpe zz"l said, "The beginning of morality is self-esteem."

Love, emotional support, and self-esteem are the primary components of spiritual health and well-being. Following this introduction, we will present a concise guide on internet filters. However, the effectiveness of internet filters is commensurate to the proper and generous nurturing of the hearts and souls – both of our children and ourselves.

Concise Guide to Internet Filters

Of course, if you can be without internet this is the safest solution.

Many educators take a realistic approach and assume the most people have internet access.

> **"If you have internet access you have a halachic obligation to install an internet filter"**
>
> - HaRav HaGaon Shmuel Vosner

That being said, no internet filter is foolproof. However, there are guidelines that help us provide ourselves with a reasonable level of protection.

Types of Internet Filters

Blacklist Filter – Blocks inappropriate sites in a few different ways. If it is generated by a secular internet provider, in most systems, it only blocks when your computer is connected to your internet provider in your home. Some blacklist filters, like K9, are installed on the computer and do block everywhere. The Torah filter systems use a combination of filters and they can provide protection from every location.

Whitelist Filter – Allows you access to all sites you choose and blocks access to all other sites. For instance, you could set it to allow your email account, your bank-account, and the train schedule – every other site is inaccessible. This is accomplished in a few different ways. If it is generated by a secular internet provider it only blocks when your computer is connected to your internet provider in your home. The strength of the whitelist system is dependent on the password holder. It can be a very strong protection, as long as the password holder is someone else who is reliable to only permit the user to select safe sites. If the user holds the password, obviously the white list filter offers zero protection. The Torah filter systems use a combination of filters and they can provide protection from every location.

Internet Filter Systems

Content Filter – Scans sites and blocks whole page or part of the page of inappropriate content.

Computer Filtering System or Mobile Filtering System – This filter is installed on the device and filters content from whatever internet connection the device accesses. This is only way to protect smartphones, laptops, or tablets, which can access public wi-fi.

- webchaver.org

- thefilternet.com

- getk9.com

Cloud Filter

- venishmartem.com/vcf - This is a white listing filter with an important innovation. The control to site selection is not in the hands of the computer user. He gives the control to a kosher filter company like, "venishmartem." In order to change sites he must contact the professionally trained staff who will advise him.

Kosher Internet Provider: Filters the internet before it reaches your home. Any computer connected in your home is protected from inappropriate sites and cannot usually be bypassed. Nor, can you access any site not offered by the service. However, a portable computer is not protected if connected to different, unprotected connection. Therefore, each computer should have an internal filter and\or a accountability solution.

Contact:

- thejnet.com

- yeshivanet.com

- koshernet.com

- vocatech.com

Accountability Solutions – This is not a filter but is very effective when used in combination with a filter. The accountability solution program sends a report of your internet activity to another person. This sharing of your information is an important way of keeping yourself honest.

- Convenanteyes.com

Phones:

- ikosher@yeshivanet.com

- bebkesher.com

Important Note: The danger of all these filters is that you have the control to regulate or remove the filter. You can easily fool yourself into thinking you are protected by your filter. In truth, you may have allowed yourself access to every inappropriate site!

May Hashem protect you and all Klal Yisrael, as King David said (Tehillim 121): "Hashem will guard you from all evil; He will preserve your soul. Hashem will guard your going and coming from now and forever."

A Quick Review

(1) Know that if you sincerely want to achieve self-mastery, Hashem will surely help you.

(2) Resolve to practice the laws of *Shmirat Einayim* for your own protection and to enhance your marriage.

(3) Throw off the burden of your *aveirot* and start over. Hashem gives everyone another chance!

(4) Each time you control your eyes from looking at an improper sight, tell yourself, "I am a member of a holy nation."

(5) Set up the first line of defense to mastering your eyes by dedicating daily time to Torah study.

(6) Be encouraged by knowing that through Mussar and *halachah* study you have the means to control your eyes and change old habits.

(7) Know that like every law in the Torah, the laws of *Shmirat Einayim* were designed for real people, just like you. Resolve to review these laws periodically in order to strengthen your observance of them.

(8) Defer to the wisdom of the Torah regarding the laws of *Shmirat Einayim*. They are relevant to every generation and every circumstance.

(9) Remember that desire will intensify in order to drown out the voice of reason. Understand that and listen closely to your soul.

(10) Use a balanced approach — understand that the laws of *Shmirat Einayim* do not allow you to deny women respect and consideration.

(11) Make a commitment to study Mussar each day for about twenty minutes.

(12) Take a few minutes in the evening to review your conduct for that day.

(13) If you must be in an area of immodestly dressed women, keep your eyes lowered and distract yourself with something worthwhile.

(14) Make a conscious effort to keep your gaze below eye-level when you are in a public place.

(15) Practicing lowering your gaze, keeping in mind that it is part of your new commitment to achieve control over your eyes.

(16) Be patient with yourself! Take a look at the mistakes you've made, so you will be alert to these specific challenges in the future.

(17) Remember that society bombards us with indecent images, so prepare yourself before you leave home.

(18) Consider the advantages of modest dress at the workplace and work to have them implemented.

(19) Remember that by cutting off improper thoughts just once, you begin a new habit of control.

(20) Respect the privacy of others by controlling your desires.

(21) Be aware of the enticing forces surrounding you. Guard your eyes from the images that try to manipulate your senses.

(22) Put the story of Mike and Gail into your mental arsenal to serve as an effective deterrent to viewing improper sights.

(23) Take steps to control the spiritual atmosphere of your home. Make your home a fitting place to receive the *Shechinah*.

(24) Help your children and future generations by controlling your eyes. Grant them "a spiritual inheritance" empowering them with the capability to preserve the well-being of their souls.

(25) Think about your heritage and internalize its meaning. Along with your awareness of Hashem and Mussar study of the Wisdom of the World, it will help you in your battle for *Shmirat Einayim*.

(26) Take the opportunity to look at holy sights and know that your soul is uplifted by them.

(27) Show this guidebook to a friend and offer to sudy it with him.

(28) Reinforce your resolve to guard your eyes in public places and know that you will receive a special blessing from G-d for your efforts.

(29) Draw closer to Hashem — now and forever — by controlling your eyes. Internalize the idea that your soul is benefitting from your restraint, whether or not you sense it.

(30) Reflect on how fortunate you are to be Jew and infuse every *mitzvah* with joy!

Bibliography

Ohr Yisrael, Rabbis Yisrael Salanter and Yitzchak Blazer

Shulchan Aruch, Even HaEzer

Taharat HaKodesh, Rabbi Aaron Rotah

Mesilat Yesharim, Rabbi Moshe Chaim Luzzato

Hilchot Isur Hestaklut B'Nashim, The Poskei HaDor

Yisrael Kadoshim, Rabbi Yisrael David Herpanas

Kedushat Einayim, Rabbi Aaron Twisig

Chut Shani, Rabbi Nissim Karelitz

Kedushat HaChaim, Rabbi Aaron Chaim Neshri

Ha'Er Eineinu, Rabbi Yoseph Shlomo Goldshmidt

Michtav M'Eliyahu, Rabbi Eliyahu Dessler

General Sponsorships

Alan Tobias
Anonymous
Baruch Amiri
Behzad Noorani
Carey Sutton
Deal Tennis Tournament
Elie Marcus
Jack Adjmi Family Foundation
Joe Rahmani
Joseph Faham
Mehrdad & Miriam Sharifian
Moise Hafez — Leiluy Nishmat Itkhak ben Sofia
Mr and Mrs David Shweky
Murray Dana
Rabbi Shaul Dayan
Richie Adjmi
Ricky Cohen
Vandale Industries